100 easy recipes to prepare on a budget, in tiny kitchens,
with dull knives, microwaves, and distractions
while earning a degree!

THE COLLEGE MAN'S
C O O K B O O K

by George Hirsch, Jr.

with Carrie Hirsch

Photographs by Butch Hirsch

thecollegemanscookbook.com

Follow us on [f] @ www.facebook.com/CollegeMansCookbook/

Follow us on [Instagram] @ www.instagram.com/thecollegemanscookbook

Follow us on [Twitter] @CollegeMansCB

Logo & Cookbook Layout by Sherri Lonz with Sherri Design

FIRST PRINTING 2017

ISBN-10:154439328 (domestic)
ISBN-13: 978-1544039329 (international)

The College Man's Cookbook

DEDICATION

I would like to dedicate this book to a couple of people but I must mention my Mom first and foremost. I learned most, if not all, of the things in the kitchen from her and she has been the most integral part to make this book a real possibility. Thank you for putting so much time and effort into making the cookbook real and also for everything else that you do on a day-to-day basis.

I would also like to dedicate this book to my Dad. Every photo that you see in this book was done by him. I don't think there are many people that could convince me to get on a dinosaur ride outside of a grocery store in public. Then on top of that, to convince me to be photographed riding it, but somehow he did. Again, this book (or me wouldn't be possible without you!

I would like to thank all my friends who helped us with this project. From testing all the recipes for my Mom and me to modeling for cookbook photos! Lastly, but definitely not least, I would like to thank Sarah. I wish that I had photos of you standing on top of the stool trying to get a good overhead view of me cutting up onions and messing up my lines way too many times. Thank you!

FOREWORD

by Jesse Blanco

Every college graduate out there, and even those who didn't graduate, can tell a story or two about the food they ate most often while they matriculated. For the record, that might be the only time I have ever use the word 'matriculated' in a sentence. It fit, so let's run with it. Personally, my go-to "meal" for lack of a better description was a bean burrito - extra cheese - from Taco Bell. There was one located right before I got on the highway after class which made it uber convenient, long before we knew what Uber would become today.

The itch to prepare my own meals instead didn't come until long after my college days were over. Was time a factor there? Perhaps. Was a lack of knowledge on how to prepare fresh and tasty meals at home between classes likely the largest obstacle to clear? More than likely it was. Most cookbooks in those prehistoric days, long before Google and smart phones replaced the Dewey Decimal, were dedicated to big, elaborate meals. Some cookbooks offered lighter versions of some classics, but the cookbook movement hadn't really trickled down to the everyday man or woman, boy or a girl. Of course, now we know times have changed.

Had their existed a *College Man's Cookbook* back in the late 1980s or early 90s, the culinary bug might have bitten me sooner than it did. Of course, we are all much older now, and those of us who love to cook get excited at the site of fresh fruits and vegetables. But I often find myself wondering *what if?*

What if there was a resource that would have kept me from burning money unnecessarily at all kinds of fast food spots? What if there was a fun book to flip through that would entice me to make a smaller version of that dish the guy made on TV the other day? What if I invited all of the guys over for the game next weekend, charge them each 5 bucks, prepared a huge kick-ass tailgate meal and still profited a few bucks? And what if I could've had a date over and totally impressed her with my culinary skill? Long before I knew that you can't just substitute whole wheat flour for regular in that pizza recipe. Don't do that. Please don't do that.

George Hirsch, Jr. is out in front of all this with his book The *College Man's Cookbook*. I've known George and his family for a couple of years, and I witnessed the passion behind the idea, I've shared and some of the conversations regarding the methodical research and finally I've seen the execution that has gone into creating really the first cookbook of its kind. At least that I have seen anyway.

The recipes in this book are simple, but creative. Some of them are pretty basic and user-friendly, a few might just inspire you to do something more with your Taco Tuesday. Any novice in the kitchen should take a copy to school with him. Moms should slip one in to their child's bag right before they head out to matriculate.

INTRODUCTION

At the time we wrote this cookbook, I was a College Man on a tight budget who loved to eat well - no better candidate to write a cookbook for College Men! We had a blast creating and testing these recipes. Eating, not necessarily eating well, is such an integral part of college life; after all, most of our bodies are still growing, no matter how many things we may do to stunt them throughout college!

One advantage I have to my credit is that I have a mother who loves cooking. We have cooked together since she put me in the baby carrier on her back while she was in the kitchen. She would be pulling maneuvers like the hibachi chefs flipping those shrimp into the top of their chef hats...and I was the hat. Nothing much has changed except she can't fit me in the baby carrier anymore! Since then, I have tried everything from the famous college downtown hot dog stands, the fattest burrito you've ever seen, gyros, very questionable 2 a.m. egg rolls, tamales, tacos, kebabs, pierogies, schnitzel, bagels, pain au chocolat, latkas, soup dumplings...you get the point.

During college, the "kitchen" I shared with my five roommates, yes, count them, five roommates, in our Junior and Senior year, consisted of a "counter" attached to the wall by some makeshift brackets which resulted in the "counter" being on an incline. It served no purpose other than to take up precious kitchen space and serve as the beer pong table during parties. The floor sagged and creaked so there was no chance of trying to enter the kitchen quietly as the floor announced to the rest of the world where I was at all times. Since the building was built in the late 1880's and was never intended to serve as an apartment building for College Men - the configuration of our kitchen was no more than a hallway with enough room for a small fridge, a dishwasher and an antique stove. The stove top had rusty coils which had their way of smoking when in use. Decades of baked-on tidbits were cemented into the nooks and crannies of the oven which ran at least one hundred degrees hotter than the knob promised. The dish washer would have been a lifesaver had it not been 2 feet wide or Beckmann not filled it with normal soap every night so it would overflow with bubbles!

In conclusion, I guess all I'm trying to say is that I have some experience in what it's like cooking on a budget, in a tiny ass kitchen, with way too many bodies in there, while still producing something you can post on social media. So take some of the recipes and tips in here and impress some friends (and probably yourself) with them!

George Hirsch, Jr.

TABLE OF CONTENTS

TABLE OF CONTENTS

RECIPES

TABLE OF CONTENTS

RECIPES

SHOPPING LISTS

Pantry items: these are items that do not require refrigeration. These are the basics and it might seem like a lot of stuff BUT most of these ingredients will last you a VERY long time:

All-Purpose Flour
Baking Powder
Baking Soda
Balsamic Vinegar
Black Beans, canned
Black Pepper
Bread
Dark Brown Sugar (in a box or bag)
Chick Peas, canned
Chocolate Chips
Coffee
Cooking spray
Extra-Virgin Olive Oil
Garlic Powder
Ground Chili Powder
Ground Cumin
Ground Ginger

Pasta - Penne, Spaghetti, Macaroni, Shells
Peanut Butter
Red Beans, canned
Red Wine Vinegar
Rice
Salt
Soy Sauce
Sugar
Tea Bags
Toasted Sesame Seed Oil
Vanilla Extract
Vegetable Oil
White Vinegar

Refrigerated/Freezer items:

Barbeque Sauce
Butter
Capers
Caesar Dressing
Cheese – Cheddar, Parmesan, etc.
Cold Cuts – turkey, ham, salami, etc.
Eggs
Frozen Pizza
Hot Sauce
Ice Cubes
Jelly or Jam
Ketchup
Lemons
Limes
Mayonnaise
Mustard

Olives
Onions
Pickles
Potatoes
Ranch Dressing
Relish
Sour Cream
Spinach

EQUIPMENT

Don't let the word "equipment" scare you- you don't need anything fancy. It's just stuff that can be found in your family kitchen that you could slip in a box while nobody's looking before you leave for college... or you, College Man, can go to a store and buy the following: The pots and skillets cannot be flimsy or else everything will burn no matter what. They must have heavy bottoms. And a reminder chefs avoid using glass in their kitchens for a reason – if a glass measuring cup breaks on the counter or anywhere near food you're preparing, it becomes a safety issue!

3 knives:
  • a paring knife
  • a mid-size knife
  • mid-sized serrated knife
8" x 8" metal baking dish
9" x 2" x13" metal baking dish
Baking sheet, large with a lip
blender
bottle opener
butter dish with lid
cake pan, 10" round
can opener
cheese grater
coffee maker
cookie sheet
cutting board, medium
cutting board, small
fire extinguisher
food processor/chopper mini
forks
frying pan, large
frying pan, medium
frying pan, small
hand mixer with beaters
heavy oven-proof skillet with lid
hot-air popcorn maker
immersion blender (for soups)
knives
ladle, large
metal bowl, large
metal bowl, medium
metal whisk, medium
muffin tin, 12 cup capacity
measuring cups, plastic
measuring spoons

metal slotted spoon
metal bowl, small
metal whisk, small
panini maker
potholders/hot hands
pot with lid, large
pot with lid, medium
pot with lid, small
scissors
silverware holder (measure drawer first)
spoons
toaster
tongs
vegetable peeler
zester

Plates, Bowls, Glasses, Cups, & Utensils:
The fewer you have on hand, the fewer you have to wash. Have 4-6 of each on hand depending on how many roommates you have. Cleaning Supplies: sponges are pretty gross and spread bacteria, so keep a bunch on hand so you can replace them quickly. Anti-bacterial cleaning spray to clean the counters, sink, counter, cabinets, refrigerator and floor.

Other Supplies:
1 box sealable sandwich bags
Aluminum foil
Food film (like Saran Wrap)
Paper towels
Plastic containers for leftover

SMART FOOD SHOPPING TIPS

A key secret – in most supermarkets where they offer the "BOGO" deals (buy one, get one free), you don't have to buy 2 or 10 or however many they say you have to buy – you can buy just ONE! Double check with a cashier first just to be sure since there may be exceptions. So look for the "BOGO" specials. If you can, buy items like extra-virgin olive oil in large containers – it may be a lot to shell out initially but in the end you'll save a lot too. In some stores in the produce section, they mark down fruits and vegetables WAY DOWN like bananas, apples, oranges, limes and potatoes and other items which are getting too ripe, turning slightly brown or are less than perfect-looking – GRAB 'EM and SAVE! And don't snub the generic brands of cereals, canned goods, spices, and other staples – they might not have the celebrity on the label, but in many cases, they taste as good as the pricier one!

The Grease Catcher: the grease catcher that is slotted into the underside of our countertop griddle was overflowing with grease because of the massive amounts of bacon we were frying – the manufacturer never imagined the grease catcher capacity needed to be ten times larger! Bacon is a staple in our College Man's diet – a food group unto itself. Remember to empty it out on a regular basis and SAVE the drippings in a container in the fridge (See "Save the Bacon Fat!" on page 71)

Don't buy cracked eggs or dented cans

What's the deal with the dented can thing and why do you think dented cans go on sale? Mystery solved! Dents, no matter how small they may appear, may have punctured and penetrated the can and could allow bacteria to grow inside. Skip them, no matter how tempting a sale. And what's a little crack in an egg shell? Well, that crack allows bacteria to get inside the egg and they can go bad VERY quickly. If you are foraging in your own fridge and you find one of your eggs is cracked (and you were so careful to check at the store!), DITCH IT.

Basic rules of food safety

It all starts at the supermarket! Don't stick your raw poultry, eggs, seafood or meat anywhere near your fresh fruits and vegetables in your shopping cart. If the meat juices leak onto them, that's where you've got a problem and you're not even home yet! Then the next thing you can do to avoid cross-contamination is to wash your hands regularly while you're cooking. Let's say you're throwing together some quick burgers and you've just made the patties using your clean hands. The grill is heating up, so you open the fridge to grab a beer, then you open the dishwasher to find the opener, then you grab a few chips to tide you over and scarf them down... you have now spread bacteria from the raw hamburger on the fridge door, the dishwasher handle, the beer bottle, inside the chip bag and into your throat – you've become a champion of harmful bacteria without even realizing it! Oh, and I forgot, you texted a few people so now it's all over your phone... And forget about you (it might be too late for you now)...what about your poor innocent roommates who are just going to the fridge for a glass of milk and now the bacteria is on their hands from the fridge door? We don't want our roommates to get sick do we? The bathroom's already in such a bad state under "normal" conditions...!

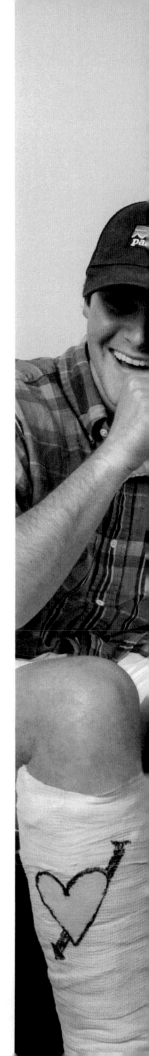

CHAPTER ONE

Breakfast & Hangover Helper

In high school, we had to wake up way too early, scarf down breakfast in a car or on a bus - breakfast was cold and your backpack weighed a ton. The idea of going to class just plain sucked. A leisurely breakfast at 4 pm, if that happens to be the time we College Men wake up, feels like sweet revenge on those painful mornings of shouting matches with parents and fights for the bathroom. The sound of an alarm clock going off was (and still is) a miserable thing and even if you threw the clock halfway across the room, the freakin' alarm still went off. Now that we use cell phones for alarms, it's easy to set at least 4 alarms a few minutes apart which is still no guarantee we're going to wake up - if we sleep through class, then we sleep through class. We now take responsibility for our irresponsibility...
In college, we have a sense of entitlement - we call the shots about what we eat for breakfast and when. Make breakfast count by being creative with these easy recipes - and always keep a jar of my Whisky Bacon Jam on hand!

Berries, Granola & Vanilla Yogurt

1 container yogurt (any size you want)
Frozen or fresh strawberries, blueberries, raspberries (one, some or all)
½ cup granola

Invert the yogurt into a serving bowl, top with fruit then granola.

Fried Eggs & Chorizo Rice

SERVES 4

1 pound raw chorizo sausage
1 tablespoon vegetable oil
1 medium onion, chopped
1 red bell pepper, diced
6 cups cooked, hot rice
½ cup any cheese, crumbled or chopped
8 eggs (2 eggs per person, or more)
½ cup fresh flat-leafed parsley, chopped
Salt and pepper

Heat oil in a heavy skillet. Place chorizo sausage in the skillet and break it up with a wooden spoon (the thin casing will easy break apart) until nicely browned. Remove chorizo from skillet and place in a bowl, leaving remaining oil in the skillet. Sauté onions and red pepper in the skillet for about 10 minutes. Add the chorizo to the onions and peppers then stir in cooked hot rice, onions, and cheese. Remove from burner, cover and set aside. Fry up your eggs. Divide chorizo rice equally into serving bowls, then top each portion with fried egg(s). Sprinkle with parsley, salt and pepper. Serve immediately.

Gone Bananas Strawberry Milk Shake

SERVES 1

1 ripe banana
Handful of ripe strawberries, stems trimmed
Handful of ice
1 cup milk
½ cup water

Process in a blender until smooth.

Ham Sliders with Creamed Eggs Gravy

In a medium skillet, heat butter over medium heat, then whisk in flour. The butter will immediately begin to absorb the flour and it will quickly thicken and become paste-like. Keep whisking it for 1 minute, then whisk in hot milk. Continue whisking until the mixture is smooth and begins to bubble, about 1 1/2 – 2 minutes. Stir in chopped hard boiled eggs. Continue to stir for 2 minutes. Cover, remove from burner then set aside for a minute. Cut each biscuit in half, spread apricot preserves on one half. Divide the ham slices to make 8 sliders. Slather with the hot creamed eggs gravy – a civilized College Man would eat this with a knife and fork but who wants to be civilized?

8 biscuits or small rolls
½ pound sliced deli ham
**2 cups creamed eggs gravy
 (recipe follows)**
**½ cup apricot preserves or
 any kind of jelly or jam**

CREAMED EGGS GRAVY:
**6 hard-boiled eggs, peeled
 and chopped**
4 tablespoons flour
4 tablespoons butter
2 cups hot milk
½ teaspoon salt
½ teaspoon black pepper

Hangover Dog

Boil, grill or fry the hot dogs. Nuke the chili and beans. The hardest part's over...now pick yourself up off the kitchen floor - you can take it from here!

2 beef hot dogs
1 medium can chili & beans
2 hot dog buns or rolls
Tabasco sauce
Mustard
Ketchup

Hollandaise Eggs & Mashed Potatoes

Peel potatoes, cut into quarters then add to a pot of cold water (enough to cover the potatoes), bring to a boil, then simmer until tender. Make sure they really are tender by piercing them with a fork-they should easily come apart. While the potatoes are cooking, make the hollandaise sauce according to package directions. Drain the potatoes, return them to the pot, then add butter, milk, salt and pepper. Mash with a potato masher or with a fork. If too dry, add more milk and butter. Cover and keep warm while you fry, scramble or poach your eggs. Divide mashed potatoes into serving bowls, top with cooked eggs, then drizzle with Hollandaise sauce.

6 medium potatoes
½ cup whole milk
Salt and pepper
**(1) .9-ounce packet Holland
 sauce mix**
1 cup milk and ½ stick butter
Eggs, as many as you like!

Nuked Cinnamon French Toast

Butter the bottom of a glass dish using your fingers. Beat together the eggs, milk and cinnamon in a medium bowl over the top. Dip bread into egg mixture then arranges slices in the bottom of the dish. Cover loosely with a damp paper towel (should not be touching the egg). Nuke for 3 minutes. Serve with syrup, more butter and fresh fruit.

1 tablespoon butter
2 eggs, beaten
2 tablespoons milk
1 teaspoon cinnamon
4 slices bread
8" glass dish
Syrup, butter and fresh fruit

Rotisserie One-Hour Chicken Soup

SERVES 2-4

1 rotisserie chicken
   (about 2 pounds)
4 cups water or as needed
Salt and pepper
Saltine crackers

Put the whole rotisserie chicken into a medium pot, then add water. I know you understand about displacement and that's why you don't put the water in the pot BEFORE you put the whole chicken in. Make sure you cut off any string or rubber bands the store might have put on it to tie it up- string will not enhance the flavors! Cover and bring to a simmer for 30 minutes. Set a large strainer over a bowl, and pour the broth and the chicken into the strainer which will leave you with the broth in the bowl below. Using a fork or your fingers (it will be hot!), pull the chicken meat off the bones and add to the bowl below. You will be left with the skin and the bones in the strainer - chuck those. If you want to keep the skin, chop it up into small pieces and add it into the soup. Salt and pepper to taste. Serve with saltines.

Shake-a-"ManGo" Smoothie

SERVES 1 HUNGRY COLLEGE MAN

1 ripe mango, peeled and
   flesh removed from pit
½ cup skim milk
½ cup Greek-style, 2% or
   fat-free yogurt
8 ice cubes

Process all ingredients in blender until smooth.

Whisky Bacon Jam

MAKES 2 CUPS

¼ cup vegetable oil
4 large onions, chopped
1 teaspoon salt
1 teaspoon black pepper
1 cup water
1 cup whiskey*this will work
   with dark rum if you're out
   of whisky
½ cup light or dark brown
   sugar
8 strips bacon, cooked crispy
   and chopped
Juice of 1 lemon
Zest of 1 lemon

Keep this on a jar in the fridge and it will last for a month or more but, trust me, it will be gone in a flash!

In a large heavy skillet, heat oil and add onions, cooking until soft and stirring often, about 10 minutes. Stir in salt, pepper, water, whisky, brown sugar, lemon juice, lemon zest, then simmer on low heat until jam begins to thicken (don't put a lid on it because you want it to cook down), stirring occasionally for about 45 minutes. If it gets too thick, add a few more teaspoons water. By the time it is finished, it will have turned a dark brown! Remove from heat then stir in chopped bacon. Once the jam begins to cool, it will thicken, even more so when it is refrigerated. Spread on toast, crackers, sandwiches, scrambled eggs, burgers, or even on cardboard if you're that desperate!

Ready, Set, Cook!

"Mise en place" is a French culinary term which simply means having all your ingredients in place before cooking to avoid scrambling at the last minute to chop or measure. It ensures a smoother process. Getting your ingredients together before you start cooking is a good idea. Pretend you have a cooking show, although you don't have a staff shopping and chopping for you, and videotape yourself for a good laugh.

Cooking is the New Golf

Yes, I agree that sounds pretty drastic but like golf or tennis, cooking can help you get in good with future spouses, bosses and in-laws. Knowing how to cook or at least making the best effort and being knowledgeable about food is key to being successful in so many ways. The man who cooks opens up his world to so much because food becomes another dimension of his character- the College Man who says "I don't cook" shuts the door on so much socially and overall. You don't have to claim to be a gourmet chef but when you start getting your grove on in the kitchen, I promise you will want to spend more time in there! You will have a passion and a talent over those who don't cook - the days of being "meat and potatoes" guys are for our grandfathers! Although nothing's wrong with a great steak and a baked spud once in a while...The soon-to-be out-in-the-real-world College Man will need to know how to impress many different people with his broad knowledge of food on a global scale. Spoiler: You don't need to be able to learn Chinese then recite ingredients in the language, brew your own beer, cure your own salami or smoke your own salmon (but that would be cool if you did though!) If this cookbook inspires you to do such things, I will be proud.

Make Food Your Business

"Oh, I have never eaten at an Indian restaurant in my life," might send the wrong message that you are not open to new types of food (or rather it might just be the case that you have not had an opportunity to do so). How is the company going to send you on assignment to Mumbai,

Tokyo, Dubai or Singapore if you might starve for fear of eating the local food? Your answer might change to "Yes, I'm a big fan of vindaloo with garlic nan and yellow lentil dahl is fantastic!" Now THAT is going to make an impression. Another benefit to cooking ethnic foods- they're CHEAP to make! Japanese? Make teriyaki chicken! Spanish? Make the paella! Mexican? Make fajitas! Chinese? Make the stir-fry! All the recipes are here in this cookbook!

Snacks To Cram By!

I can't speak for you, but when I'm cramming for tests and have to pull an all-nighter or at least a super-late-into-the-morning-hours binge study session, there are a few key things that keep me sane- my music, and my snacks. Salted roasted peanuts - the salt is key for me! Energy drinks? Um...they don't grow in trees or in a garden...I'm not exactly sure where they come from and the mystery ingredients just baffle me. Me, I would personally drink something that tastes good. Take a two-minute break and make a shake instead. In the morning or even a week before you know you'll be hitting the books hard, peel and cut up a few ripe bananas into 1-inch chunks, put them in a plastic bag and throw them in the freezer- that's just a figure of culinary speech - but throw them if it makes you feel good.

When you feel yourself trying to nestle into the crease of your textbooks for a quick nap (one that could last hours) and need a quick pick-me-up, take out a hand full of the frozen banana chunks, throw them in a blender with a huge spoonful of peanut butter (no need to exact measure here), add a cup of cold water, then process until smooth. Maybe we could try adding a shot of cold expresso and see what happens?! Drink up!

CHAPTER TWO

Appetizers & Snacks

"Appetizer" is a fancy word for foods that are supposed to start a meal and whet your appetite, College Man, but we know we don't eat "appetizers" - we eat anything that's not nailed down and we eat it all day and night. Our "snacks" might feed a family of four but for organizational purposes I started Chapter 2 with appetizers and snacks... French Language Majors call them "hors d'oeuvres". My favorite easy appetizer is, by far, lemon hummus. Making your own hummus may not have ever been on your radar, and your roommates may think Martha Stewart has invaded your body but seriously, making it from scratch tastes so much better than store-bought hummus. The one essential ingredient is tahini which is sesame seed paste and is easy to find in supermarkets in jars - I admit, it's a little pricey but it'll make a few batches. And adding the fresh lemon juice seals the deal. I guarantee, once you make your own delicious, garlicky and lemony hummus, College Man, you'll never shop in the hummus isle again.

3-Alarm Peel 'n Eat Shrimp

SERVES 2-4

**2 pounds medium shrimp
 with the shells & tails on**
⅛ cup seasoning mix
 (see recipe that follows)
½ stick butter
¼ cup hot sauce

SEASONING MIX:
**1 teaspoon black pepper or
 lemon pepper**
**1 teaspoon chili pepper,
 crushed red pepper
 or paprika**
1 teaspoon garlic powder
1 teaspoon ground ginger

Fill a large pot half way with water, then add shrimp. As you bring the water to a boil, then you will see the shrimp turning a shade of light pink, so cooking them does not take more than a few minutes. Drain and transfer to a large serving bowl. Sprinkle with butter and seasoning mix and toss to coat well.

TO MAKE A SUPER SEASONING MIX:
If you don't have all these spices, don't worry, it'll still work!

Combine all ingredients in a small bowl.

Antipasto Slider Platter

SERVES 8-10

**½ pound thinly sliced
 Genoa salami**
½ pound thinly sliced ham
**½ pound thinly sliced roast
 beef**
**½ pound thinly sliced
 mozzarella cheese**
**½ pound thinly sliced
 Provolone cheese**
½ cup black olives
½ cup green olives
**½ pound blue cheese,
 crumbled**
**24 small dinner rolls or
 biscuits for sliders**

DRESSING:
1 teaspoon garlic salt
1 teaspoon dried basil
1 teaspoon dried parsley
1 teaspoon black pepper
1 teaspoon dried oregano
**¼ cup white or red
 wine vinegar**
½ cup extra-virgin olive oil

Toothpicks

"Antipasto" means "before the meal" in Italian (if you really want to learn a foreign language, date a person who was born there or if you can study abroad there – do it!) so now you know when to serve this, but it doesn't really matter because you could eat this anytime. You can decide how much you want to serve of each, but you will be safe with a ½ pound of each of the deli meats and cheeses.

Roll up the meat and cheese slices, cut in half, and secure with toothpicks. Arrange on a serving platter, along with the olives and blue cheese. Whisk together (or put in a jar with a tight lid) all dressing ingredients. Drizzle half the dressing over items on the platter and put the remaining dressing in a little bowl next to the platter for dipping. Place the little rolls in a basket next to the platter. Cover platter and refrigerate until ready to serve. College Men will make their own sliders, of course remembering to remove ALL toothpicks before consuming...

Brutal Bruschetta

MAKES 2 ½ CUPS

Slice tomatoes ½-inch thick slices, then cut into cubes. It's OK if some of the seeds remain. Transfer to a small serving bowl. Toss in olive oil, capers, garlic, and parmesan cheese until tomato cubes are well coated. Salt and pepper to taste (if necessary). Serve on toasted bread slices, untoasted.

12 ripe Roma tomatoes
½ cup extra virgin olive oil
2 chopped and seeded jalapenos OR ½ teaspoon chipotle powder (or however much you can take)
2 tablespoons capers, drained
3 large cloves garlic, finely chopped
½ cup shredded Parmesan
Salt and pepper to taste
Toasted bread slices

Buffalo Drumsticks

SERVES 4

Preheat oven to 425°. Using your kitchen scissors, cut off the any excess fatty skin from the drumsticks or any little loose bone pieces and discard. Combine drumsticks, garlic, oil, cayenne pepper, and salt in a large bowl. Toss until well coated. Arrange in a large baking dish so they don't overlap. Sprinkle flour over drumsticks using a mesh strainer. Bake for 50 minutes, turning them over once using tongs half way through the baking time. While the drums are baking, stir together melted butter and hot sauce in a large bowl. Remove drumsticks from the oven, discard the juices, then place the baked drumsticks into the large bowl with the butter and hot sauce mixture. Toss to coat. Serve with blue cheese dressing (recipe follows) and celery sticks!

BLUE CHEESE DRESSING (MAKES ABOUT 1⅛ CUPS)
In a small bowl, mash up blue cheese with a fork, leaving it on the chunky side. Pour milk into a measuring cup, then stir in lemon juice and let it stand for 10 minutes. You will see that the milk will become thicker and will begin to curdle (you have just made a version of buttermilk!) Whisk in the now-curdled milk and sour cream. Cover and refrigerate for 1 hour. Cut up celery stalks into thin sticks. They will stay fresh in the fridge until ready to serve if you put them in a little container submerged in salty water.

4-5 pounds drumsticks
8 cloves chopped garlic or 2 tablespoons garlic powder
¼ cup vegetable oil
2 tablespoons cayenne pepper
¼ cup all-purpose flour
1 teaspoon salt
1 stick melted butter
½ cup hot sauce

DRESSING:
1 cup crumbled blue cheese
½ cup milk
1 tablespoon lemon juice or white vinegar
½ cup sour cream

Corn & Black Bean Dip

MAKES 3-4 CUPS

2 tablespoons butter
3 medium cans corn, drained
1 medium can cooked black beans, drained and rinsed
3 tablespoons balsamic vinegar
1 teaspoon sugar
3 tablespoons extra-virgin olive oil
Tortilla chips

Place the butter in a large sauté pan or skillet over medium-high heat. Add the corn and black beans, and cook until heated through, stirring occasionally. Pour mixture into a serving bowl. Stir in balsamic vinegar, sugar, olive oil, salt, and pepper. Serve warm or chilled with tortilla chips.

"Edamame" (Soy Beans)

SERVES 2

1 bag frozen edamame pods*
***bags of shelled edamame are also sold but half the fun is taking them out of the pod, but if you don't feel up to the challenge, then get the shelled ones...**
1 medium pot boiling water
Salt to taste

Have you heard of a soy bean? That's what an edamame is, in its natural form when it hasn't been turned into milk, tofu or a gazillion other foods... this is also what you may have ordered at a Japanese restaurant but not really sure what to do with. There have been witness accounts of the entire edamame pod being eaten rather than the beans being squeezed out. I have also seen someone take an already sucked on edamame pod and pop it in their mouth only to find out that they had made a big mistake.

Gently pour the frozen edamame into the boiling water or you can steam them, using a double boiler. Boil them for 10 minutes or according to the package's recommended time, remove with a slotted spoon. Transfer to a serving bowl, and sprinkle with salt. Take soy beans out of the pods and eat them.

Lemon Hummus

MAKES APPROXIMATELY 3 CUPS

Juice of 4 lemons
3-4 cloves chopped garlic
½ cup tahini which is sesame seed paste (well stirred because the oil separates)
3 cups chick peas (also known as "garbanzo beans", drained and rinsed)
½ cup extra-virgin olive oil
2 tablespoons water
1 teaspoon salt
Chopped fresh parsley, for garnish
Pita bread

Add all ingredients in a food processor or blender and process until smooth. If too thick, add more lemon juice and/or a little water. Cover and refrigerate because it will firm up when colder. When ready to serve, drizzle with a bit of olive oil and top with chopped parsley (optional). Serve with toasted pita bread or chips.

Rosemary Hummus Soft Tacos

MAKES 4 TACOS

In a small bowl, mix fresh lemon juice and hummus together with a fork. Spread hummus over flour tacos. Sprinkle with olive oil and rosemary. Roll up and eat!

4 small soft flour tacos
8 tablespoons hummus
2 teaspoons freshly squeezed lemon juice
½ teaspoon extra-virgin olive oil
½ teaspoon finely chopped fresh or dried rosemary

Spicy ManGo Salsa

MAKES 3 CUPS

Combine all ingredients in a serving bowl. Serve with tortilla chips.

2 ripe diced mangoes
2 tablespoons diced red onion
1 seeded and minced jalapeno pepper
½ bunch finely chopped cilantro leaves
2 tablespoons vegetable oil
½ teaspoon ground ginger
2 tablespoons lime juice
Tortilla Chips

Wasabi Egg Salad Melt (Open Faced)

MAKES 4 SANDWICHES

Peel and chop up the hard-boiled eggs. In a medium bowl, stir together chopped up eggs, mayonnaise, wasabi sauce, and salt and pepper. Throw it in the fridge for a few minutes, then toast bread. Put the toast on a baking sheet, then divide the wasabi egg salad between them – these are open-faced. Sprinkle with shredded cheese, then broil on high heat for 2-3 minutes, watching carefully so they don't burn. Please do not get distracted by your appetite - remember to turn off the broiler so you don't burn the place down!

4 hard-boiled eggs
2 tablespoons mayonnaise
2 tablespoons wasabi sauce
1 teaspoon salt
½ teaspoon black pepper
4 slices of bread
1 cup shredded cheese

Notes:

Cooking Pays Off in More Ways Than One

College Men tend to eat way too much fast food on a daily basis, which has major consequences – artificial colorings, preservatives, hormones, and other ingredients commonly, or mostly, used in fast food just cannot be beneficial to the College Man's mind and body. Also, based on shopping and cooking in your own kitchen, you, the College Man, have more control over the quality of your ingredients (YES, IT MATTERS!) and can save a tremendous amount of money. Think of all the money that you can save by cooking at home and think of the possibilities of what you can do with it (in random order, but not really): more beer, more ubers, more dates, more technology, or whatever makes you happy. Did I mention more money for books? It just wouldn't seem right to spend it on books...kinda spoils the satisfaction of saving it in the first place but to each his own. And, if you haven't saved a significant amount of money after using this cookbook for six months, you have simply gone off the grid and need to regroup, check your equipment list again and just start over, college man! Now there is the other scenario, where you could actually lose money because once word gets out about how great a cook you are (they don't know that it's REALLY not that big a deal, people!), roommates of roommates, ex-partners, one night stands, absentee parents, the building's maintenance staff and complete strangers will be popping in to experience it for themselves-hopefully they will be very smart, good-looking and know how to wash dishes.

The Nose Test

You will easily pass this test, but, sorry, it will not raise your GPA, College Man. You simply cannot trust an expiration date on a package of highly perishable items like meat, poultry, fish and other seafood. Once I cracked an egg that was bad into a frying pan, and trust me, I knew immediately that is was rotten by the smell, the color and overall appearance, more like a jellyfish from hell. Once you open a package, take a quick sniff and use your best judgement. If it smells off or you're not quite sure if it's fresh, dump it. Cooking something that's spoiled will not magically transform it into something good. It will just be something that's bad, but now it's cooked. Gross.

Dumb Things We Don't Admit to Doing

That last piece of toast was stuck in the toaster and so you took a fork to dislodge it...seriously, you could get a major shock from an appliance! The better way might be to *unplug it* then try to dislodge it without damaging the toaster. And if you accidentally cut yourself while practicing your knife skills to the point where you need stitches, make your way to the emergency room! Good news: Even the best cooks cut themselves once in a while. Bad news: you might even need a tetanus shot. The scar will give you something to brag about...

Broaden Your Brews

Ninety-nine bottles of beer on the wall,
Ninety-nine bottles of beer,
Take one down and pass it around,
Ninety-eight bottles of beer on the wall...

Naturally, learning about beer has the added benefit of drinking beer, so since there are thousands of beers out there, why stick with the same beer every time? You could easily try a new one every day of the year, or however often you drink beer, which we assume, College Man, is daily. It's easy to drink the same old beer but since variety is the spice of life, but why not venture out to sample different brews? Breweries are opening up in college towns all over the country in record numbers. Beer is a fermented, carbonated drink brewed from water, grains and yeast. Simple, right? Brew masters will tell you otherwise. Are you a beer aficionado who appreciates the difference between ale and lager and what "finishing gravity" and "lagering" have to do with brewmasters' techniques or do you chase a few beers with friends without it giving your choice of brew much thought? Here's a short tutorial: beer comes in many colors: blond, golden, copper, dark brown, bronze, orange, pink, and black- even red, and white and blue. In terms of appearance, a beer looks either transparent, translucent, or opaque. Flavors span the spectrum from oatmeal, chocolate, and caramel, to banana, malt, and pear. Beer can have nutty or subtle smoky aromas and can be spiced up with cinnamon and other spices and even with herbs like sage and rosemary. Where are those darn ping pong balls?

CHAPTER THREE
Soups, Stews & Chowders

The poster child for college life: envision the starving college student (starving maybe because we didn't have the foresight to shop?) with a stack of packages of chicken and beef flavored ramen noodles on the counter and nothing else. Does this sound familiar? What if you could transform the ramen noodles? Like you're giving them a total make-over show and at the end, the ramen noodles walk down the stairs and the family and friends (in this case it's you and your roommates) start to cheer and cry because the ramen noodles they once knew – salt laden, sometimes soggy noodles, have become a colorful, textured and delicious new and improved ramen noodles? Here's how it's done, and if you're skeptical about it, just try it and then you'll end up creating your own version with just a few new ingredients.

Bacon Cheeseburger n' Fries Soup

SERVES 6

1 large chopped onion
1 tablespoon vegetable oil
2 pounds ground beef
8 cups beef broth
3 medium potatoes, peeled
    and cut into small French
    fry shapes
Salt & pepper to taste

TOPPINGS:
1 cup potato chips
6 slices cheddar cheese or 1
    cup grated cheddar cheese
1 cup sautéed mushrooms
8 fried and chopped strips
    bacon
Ketchup
Sweet or Sour Pickle Chips

In a soup pot, heat oil and sauté onions on medium heat until soft, stirring frequently, about 10 minutes. Add ground beef, chop up with spoon while browning, about 15 minutes. Add beef broth and potato fries. Bring to a boil, then turn down heat, cover and simmer for 30 minutes. Salt and pepper to taste.

Assembly: ladle into individual serving bowls. Add cheese first because it needs to melt, then top with bacon, onion slices, ketchup, pickles, mushrooms, chips any other toppings you like!

Corn Chowder to Chow On

SERVES 6-8

4 tablespoons butter
1 medium finely diced onion
4 medium-size cans white or
    yellow corn, undrained or use
    a large bag of frozen kernels
1 red bell pepper, diced into
    ¼" pieces
6 medium potatoes, diced
    into 1/2" chunks
3 cups vegetable or chicken
    broth
2 cups half and half (OK to
    use heavy cream, whole milk,
    skim or a combination)
Salt and pepper to taste
Large handful parsley finely
    minced cilantro, stems
    discarded

GARNISH:
Fresh or canned jalapeno
    pepper slices
4 strips cooked, diced bacon

In large pot, over medium heat, melt butter. Add onions and sauté for 5 minutes, until softened, stirring often. Add corn, red pepper, potatoes, broth, salt and pepper, and sauté for 10 minutes. Add half and half, then bring to a boil. Turn heat down to low, add parsley, and simmer, covered, for 20 minutes or until potatoes are tender. If you want to thicken up the chowder, use an immersion blender or transfer half the chowder to a food processor, then lightly puree mixture to desired consistency, leaving some potatoes whole. Serve in bowls and sprinkle with jalapeños and/or bacon.

French Onion Soup

SERVES 4

¼ cup vegetable oil
8-10 medium chopped onions
2 large vegetable, chicken or beef bouillon cubes
4 cups water
½ cup white wine
1 teaspoon black pepper
4 slices buttered bread
1½ cups grated Gruyere or Swiss cheese
Salt and pepper to taste

In a large heavy pot, heat the oil over medium heat then add the onions. Test if the oil is hot enough by putting in a piece of the chopped onion – if it sizzles, it is ready. If the piece just sits there motionless, like some people I have known, the oil is not ready. Stir the onions frequently. They need to cook to the point where they begin to caramelize and start to turn a light shade of brown. Be patient and it will happen after about 1 hour of cooking-keep the pot covered for 15 minutes, then uncover for the remaining 45 minutes. The onions will cook down while most of the liquid inside the onions cooks out. Towards the end of the cooking time, make sure to stir a lot or they may burn on the bottom. Pour 4 cups water into a glass bowl with the 2 vegetable bouillon cubes, then nuke until for 3 minutes. Using a fork, break up any bouillon cubes which have not completely dissolved.

Pour vegetable broth, wine and black pepper into the pot with the onions then stir, cover, and simmer on low heat for 15 minutes. Taste to see if it needs salt and pepper, taking into account the cheese (which will be the final step) will bring some salty flavor to the soup. Toast the buttered bread in the oven at 350 degrees or you can broil them. Depending on your broiler, it can take less than 30 seconds, so don't get distracted and turn off that broiler! Spoon the soup into individual soup bowls, lay a slice of toasted buttered bread on top. Sprinkle the shredded cheese between the bowls and nuke until cheese melts. Serve immediately. Did you really turn off the broiler?

Since you've got the main course under control, your friends can bring the drinks and dessert!

Frogmore Stew

Serves 6-8

Water
½ cup Old Bay Seasoning
2 teaspoons salt
4 ears corn on the cob
2 pounds kielbasa *(comes pre-cooked)*
6 red-skinned potatoes, washed and unpeeled
2 pounds peeled medium shrimp

Ok, I'll tell you upfront-this is not a true stew and there are NO slimy frogs in here...it is also known as Lowcountry Boil!

Fill a large pot half full with water. Add Old Bay seasoning and salt and bring water to a boil. Cut ears of corn into thirds. Slice kielbasa into ½" pieces. Cut potatoes into quarters. Add potatoes, corn and kielbasa to the pot. Return to a gentle boil, cover and cook until potatoes are done (about 15-20 minutes), adding additional Old Bay seasoning if desired. When potatoes are cooked, add shrimp and simmer for 3-4 more minutes or until shrimp turn light pink. Drain out all the liquid and serve with cocktail sauce.

"Kick A Cold in the Butt" Spicy Soup

SERVES 4

3 tablespoons vegetable or coconut oil
1 chopped medium onion
1 tablespoon crushed red pepper flakes
6 chopped cloves garlic*
4 cups chicken or vegetable broth
Juice of 2 limes
Zest of 2 limes
2 chopped green onions (these are the long and skinny, held together with a rubber band in the produce section white at the base and green towards the top, also known as scallions)
Chopped parsley
Salt & pepper to taste

If your nose runs when you're eating this soup you've made it the way you're supposed to!

Heat oil in a heavy pot over low heat. Sauté onions and garlic over low-medium heat until soft, stirring frequently. Add chili flakes and stir for 1 minute. Add chicken broth and bring to a simmer. Cover and simmer on low heat for 10 minutes. Remove from the heat and stir in lime juice, lime zest, green onions and parsley. Salt and pepper to taste. Slurp HOT!

*(garlic trivia: each "head" of garlic has about 10-12 cloves in it)

Optional: if you have any cooked chicken, shrimp, pork, fish or tofu, you can add it in during the last stage of the simmering!

Ramen Noodles Renaissance

If you add fresh herbs (dried won't work) and other ingredients to your ramen noodles, you will transform them: the key is whatever you choose must be chopped fine because you add it after you have actually cooked the ramen noodles according to the package directions, and then allow it to simmer for 3 minutes, then turn it off and let it sit for 3 more minutes and you're done. By chopping it fine, whatever you are adding is slightly cooked but still has some crunch to it without getting soggy. Also, once you start to add other ingredients, add ½ cup more water otherwise it will be too thick.

Choose 1, 2 or 3 of these in any combination and your ramen noodles will come to life! You can use as many as you like: Fresh chopped green chilies (cut out the stems and seeds), chopped green onions (start chopping from the white part at the base but stop chopping when the green part gets too tough), chopped cilantro, shredded carrots, chopped parsley, chopped raw beets (yes, raw) chopped spinach, chopped tomatoes, chopped zucchini and/or bean sprouts! Top with roasted salted peanuts!

Spicy Black Bean Soup with Sweet Potato Puree

SERVES 10

OK, fine, it's bean soup –just be polite please! This is our friend's Gavin & Holly's recipe-we love it!

In a very large pot, add black beans, then add water. If you see any misshapen beans or anything that shouldn't be in there floating on the surface of the water, just pick it out. Stir in onion, garlic, and salt. Cover and bring to a boil, then lower heat so that it is at a medium simmer, stirring occasionally. Keep covered, and simmer on low heat for 2 hours, or until beans are soft. Remove 2 cups of cooked beans and puree in a mini food processor or smash with a fork. Return pureed beans to the pot and stir. Add salsa and stir. Salt and pepper to taste.

To make the sweet potato puree, discard skin from sweet potato then place in a small bowl. Mash with a fork. If too dry, add a few drops of water or milk. To make the sour cream sauce, in a small bowl, whisk together sour cream, mayonnaise and water.

To serve, place bean soup in individual bowls, add a dollop of mashed sweet potato then drizzle with sour cream sauce in a zig zag pattern.

SOUP:
(3) 16-ounce packages dried black beans
21 cups water
1 large yellow onion, finely chopped
12 garlic cloves, finely chopped
2 teaspoons salt
3 cups spicy tomato salsa
Salt & pepper to taste

SWEET POTATO PUREE:
2 large sweet potatoes, baked in 375° oven for 1 hour or until done (*pierce with a fork before baking so they don't explode!*)

SOUR CREAM SAUCE:
4 tablespoons sour cream
2 tablespoons mayonnaise
4 teaspoons water

Spicy Chorizo & Drunken Rice Soup

SERVES 4

Heat oil in a heavy skillet. Using scissors, remove chorizo from the sausage casing (throw casing away) and brown over low heat for 10 minutes, chopping it up with a spatula as you go. If it gets too dry and starts to stick to the skillet, add 1/2 cup of the chopped tomato juices. Add diced tomatoes, garlic, vegetable broth, red wine, salt and pepper. Cover and simmer for 20 minutes over low heat, stirring occasionally. Cook the rice according to package directions. Divide the rice between serving bowls, and top with the chorizo soup. Garnish with chopped green onions and sour cream.

1 pound raw chorizo sausages (*about 3-4 links*)
1 tablespoon vegetable oil
1 (28-ounce) can diced tomatoes, in their juices
6 cloves chopped garlic
2 cups vegetable or chicken broth
1 cup red wine or ½ bottle dark beer
Salt and pepper to taste
6 cups cooked hot rice

Spud & Bacon Chowder

SERVES 4-6

½ pound bacon
1 chopped onion
2 1/2 tablespoons flour
3 cups vegetable or
    chicken broth
3-4 potatoes
2 cups milk (or 1 cup milk
    and 1 cup half and half for a
    richer chowder)
Salt and pepper to taste

This is optional - but if you want to add chopped ham during the last few minutes of cooking, that'll work!

In a large, heavy pot fry the bacon, then remove the bacon onto a cutting board. Keep the fat from the bacon in the pot, then add the chopped onion.

Over low heat, sauté the onions until translucent and be sure to stir them every couple of minutes. Peel and cut potatoes into ½" cubes (about 3 cups). Pour in the flour and broth and stir so the flour doesn't clump up. Chop up and stir in bacon then add potato cubes, Stir and cover, bring to a boil, then summer on low heat for 15 minutes- the way you will know it is done is by trying the potatoes - they will be cooked through. Make sure you stir the pot a few times as it simmers- if it seems too thick add ½ cup water or vegetable broth. Stir in the salt, pepper and milk (and chopped ham if you are adding any). Simmer for 2 more minutes and serve. May need additional salt and pepper to taste!

Turkey Chili

SERVES 4

1½ pounds ground turkey
1 tablespoon vegetable oil
1 chopped onion
4 cloves chopped garlic
1 bottle dark beer
2 cans red or pink beans,
    drained and rinsed
1 medium can diced tomatoes
    (keep in the liquid)
1 tablespoon ground cumin
1 tablespoon chili powder
Salt and pepper to taste

In a medium pot, heat oil. Sauté onions and garlic until soft, then add ground turkey to pot, chopping it up with a spatula as it browns, stirring often. Add beer, beans, diced tomatoes, cumin and chili powder, and bring to a simmer. Cover and simmer for 20-25 minutes on low heat. Salt and pepper to taste. Top with sour cream, chopped green onions and cheddar cheese.

Find Your Inner 'Iron Chef'

Your worst nightmare: it's snowing, you have no gas in the tank (literally and figuratively), it's 1 AM and you're starving. Terrified, you head for the kitchen to see if there are any crumbs, anything that is still remotely edible and the results are dismal ...pickles, crusty three-day old rice, an egg, a bag of frozen vegetables (a good chance it has freezer burn but it won't kill you) from last semester and an onion. There are some packs of soy sauce that have remained on the kitchen counter, untouched, from last year. One day, (tonight, actually), they would serve a purpose. You've watched millions of episodes of "Iron Chef" (the Japanese version with subtitles?) and find it within yourself to step up to the challenge, although there are no cameras or lights on you, no annoying make-up person dabbing your nose and combing your greasy hair – nothing to distract you from creating a miracle. You steam the crusty rice by adding a little water and covering it for a few minutes. Like Frankenstein, it springs back to life! You then nuke the frozen vegetables according to the package directions. In a skillet, you heat a touch of oil, then chop up the onion and sauté it. You scoop out the onions, set them in a bowl, and then heat a few drops more oil. You beat then scramble the egg, chop it up and add it to the bowl of onions. You heat a few more drops of oil, stir fry the hot veggies and rice, then add in the onions and chopped egg. You drizzle your masterpiece with soy sauce! Your eyes are brimming with tears with pride or because you're so damn happy to have something to eat... Your roommate arrives as you finish the last bite and all that's left are the pickles. Sorry, Bro.

No Raw Meat

For those of you who think it's cool to eat raw hamburger or any type of raw eggs, it's NOT cool - don't think about eating even ONE tiny bite of raw meat! I don't even want to tell you about the evil microbes that could be lurking in there just waiting to invade your body and I'm not even a Food Science Major. When you place raw meat on any plate or on your cutting board to prepare it for cooking, be sure to NEVER put the cooked meat back on the same plate. And if you marinate meat or chicken before cooking, don't add that marinade back into it or you will

have a BACTERIAFEST! Also, it's better to use your cutting board to make your salads FIRST before using it for perishable foods (like meat), just to be sure you're not contaminating your salad.

Hamburger and Turkey Meat

When buying hamburger meat, avoid chuck and go for lean "ground round". When it's on sale, it can be the same price as ground chuck but you will have a better tasting burger using the ground round. You can make a turkey burger in the same way you make a hamburger. There is a choice of ground white turkey meat and ground dark turkey meat in the package but if you go to the butcher counter, you can buy 1 pound of each (or equal quantities depending on how much you need) and then you can combine them to make your turkey burger moist. Get to know your butcher and ask him or her questions. If you get the 100% white turkey meat, your turkey burger will be super lean and will cook much faster than a beef hamburger, so don't overcook it and make it into a hockey puck.

Recipes Gone Wrong: Baked Potatoes

We all know it can happen! That's what happens when distractions have their way with you, College Man. An NBA final, a text from a buddy, falling asleep or all of the above can sabotage cooking...there's such a thing as trying to save time and then there's plain stupidity. I nuked a potato in the microwave once and it exploded into a million pieces with a nuclear "boom". Science Majors refer to this as "combustion"...There are many uses for microwaves but baking potatoes is not one of them - if I had made little holes with a knife or a fork everything would have been fine except for one thing- the texture would still have been gummy and the potato would not have the delicious crusty skin. The moral of the story is to bake your potato in a preheated oven at 400° for about 45 minutes, but first wash it, dry it with a paper towel, rub it with a teaspoon of extra-virgin olive oil and sprinkle it with a pinch of coarse salt and black pepper. Your potato goes right on the oven rack. Set your timer so those distractions don't sabotage your potato this time!

CHAPTER FOUR

Burgers, Sandwiches, Rolls & Tacos

Sinking your teeth into a really good sub is the best, right? Sweet Italian sausages with onions and green peppers make up the addictive flavors in my "Bad-Ass Godfather" Super Bowl Sub, but you can make it all year round- no need for a testosterone fest to make it!

A great burger hits the spot every time - I opted for the twist of dropping a burger between toasted waffles and we made another burger recipe with wasabi- the green spicy condiment you eat with sushi. And if you do drop a burger on the floor, the 10-second rule applies here (I've added 5 more seconds to the old 5-second rule just because). If you don't even know with the 5- second rule is then chances are pretty good you're a germaphobe, so go ahead and disregard those rules.

This chapter is meat-chicken-fish oriented but if you're not a carnivore, you can substitute hot or cold grilled vegetables for most of the recipes! And remember, if you don't have every single ingredient, don't worry about it. Improvising and making do with what you have on is part of learning how to cook, although making a hamburger without hamburger meat is impossible.

BLT with a Kick!

MAKES 2 SANDWICHES

2 pieces sliced bread or
   hamburger buns
8 fried strips bacon
Washed lettuce leaves
1 large sliced ripe tomato
Salt and pepper to taste

CHIPOTLE MAYONNAISE:
¼ cup mayonnaise
1 teaspoon chipotle powder

Spread inside bread slices with chipotle mayonnaise. Layer the bacon, lettuce, and tomato. Salt and pepper to taste.

Chicken Parm in the Oven

SERVES 6

6 chicken boneless chicken
   breasts *(about 2 ½ pounds)*
2 tablespoons extra virgin
   olive oil
½ teaspoon salt
½ teaspoon pepper
½ teaspoon garlic powder
½ teaspoon dried basil
24-ounce jar spaghetti sauce
1 cup finely grated
   parmesan cheese
1 pound shredded mozzarella
6 Italian rolls

Preheat oven to 375°. Toss chicken breasts with olive oil, salt, pepper, garlic powder and dried basil in a medium bowl. In grill pan or in heavy skillet, over medium heat, grill chicken breasts until golden brown and each side, about 8 minutes total. Chicken will not be cooked through, but will finish cooking in oven. Pour spaghetti sauce into a 9" x 13" x 2" dish, and spread around to cover bottom of pan. Place grilled chicken in rows on top of sauce. Sprinkle parmesan evenly over chicken, then top with shredded mozzarella. Cover with foil and bake for 20 minutes. Remove foil and turn broiler on, and finish by broiling for 2-3 minutes until cheese is lightly browned and bubbling. Remove from oven and place Italian rolls in the oven for 3 minutes or until toasted. Divide chicken parmesan equally onto toasted Italian rolls.

Gone Fishin' Tacos (Baked)

Sprinkle mahi-mahi steaks with blackening mix. In a large, heavy skillet, heat oil and sauté for 5 minutes a side over medium-high heat. Warm the taco shells in the oven on a cookie sheet for 3-4 minutes at 350°. Serve with warmed taco shells and all the fixings.

4 pounds boneless fish filets, 1-inch thick (about 2 pounds any fish you like)
2 tablespoons blackening mix (see recipe below)
1 tablespoon olive oil
½ cup salsa
½ head shredded lettuce
2 chopped ripe tomatoes
½ diced red onion
Sour cream
Hot sauce
(8) hard taco shells or flour tortillas

TO MAKE BLACKENING MIX:

If you don't have all of these spices, don't worry, it'll still work as a delicious blackening mix!

Combine all ingredients in a small bowl.

TO MAKE BLACKENING MIX:
½ teaspoon black pepper
½ teaspoon chili pepper
½ teaspoon dried basil
½ teaspoon dried oregano
½ teaspoon garlic powder
½ teaspoon ground thyme

Ham & Cheese Rolls

Preheat oven to 350°. Arrange dinner rolls and place in a baking dish – the closer they are together the better and it's OK for them to touch. Top with chopped ham, cheese slices, syrup, garlic salt and sweet relish. Whisk together melted butter and mustard and drizzle over rolls. Cover with foil and bake for 12-15 minutes.

12 soft dinner rolls
¼ pound sliced deli ham, chopped
¼ pound sliced cheese
2 tablespoons pancake syrup, honey or agave
½ teaspoon garlic salt
2 tablespoons sweet relish

TOPPING:
½ cup melted butter
3 tablespoons Dijon-style mustard

Roast Beef Sandwiches Au Jus

1 tablespoon extra-virgin olive oil
1 tablespoon butter
1 large chopped onion
4 cups beef bouillon
1 pound sliced deli roast beef
Salt and pepper to taste
8 slices provolone, Swiss or Gruyere cheese (*2 slices per hoagie*)
4 hoagie rolls

(*"au jus" means in the juices, meaning the juices for dunking*)

Preheat oven to 400°. In a small skillet, heat oil and butter, then sauté onions until soft, stirring often. Cover and set aside. In a medium pot, heat beef bouillon then add roast beef slices, salt and pepper and simmer for 2 minutes. Turn off the heat and cover the pot while you prepare the rolls. Cut the hoagies in half lengthwise and lay them on a cookie sheet until lightly browned, about 5-8 minutes. Keep the oven on because you will need the broiler in a little while.

Assembling the hoagies: set aside the top halves and spread the caramelized onions on the toasted bottom halves. Take the roast beef slices out of the beef bouillon and place over the caramelized onions, then place the cheese slices on top. Turn the oven to "broil" setting, then place in oven on the middle rack, then broil, watching carefully, until the cheese melts. Remove the hoagies, press the top halves down on top. Pour the warm beef broth into 4 individual bowls (not one communal bowl in case of...ya know) and dunk away!

TIDBITS AND TASTY THOUGHTS

Spaghetti Test

Some say that the real way to eat spaghetti or any pasta is "al dente" (which translates from Italian as "to the tooth") but we think it is a matter of personal choice. There is a method that is fun and entertaining at the same time. To test if your spaghetti is done, throw a few pieces up against the wall or ceiling and if they stick, the spaghetti is done! This does not apply to other pasta like macaroni because no matter how done it is, if you throw macaroni up against a wall it will fall to the ground. After retrieving the spaghetti from the wall (if you choose to do so – otherwise consider it art?), taste it anyway, because it may need another minute or two in the boiling water.

Pasta the Right Way

Pasta. The staple to most College Men's kitchen. It's cheap, it tastes good with red sauce and Parmesan, it's pretty easy to make, and oh did I mention that it's cheap? There are so many great and go-to recipes that are centered around pasta that it is very important that you know how to cook it the right way. It can make or break your dish. Here's the thing about pasta, though. You gotta pay attention.You can't just throw some of it in water in a pot and let it boil for 10-12 minutes. There's a process to making sure that your pasta is not only edible, but tastes good, too. Depending on how much pasta you're making, some of this will differ like the size of the pot, amount of water, etc. but this is safe for a serving of 2-4 people depending on who's eating.

Bring a pot of water to a boil (it will say exactly how much water you will need on the box of pasta). Salt the water before it boils (adds flavor). Pour in pasta. Immediately stir pasta so that individual pieces don't stick or clump together. Stir it every 30 seconds for the first few minutes. This will ensure that no pasta sticks together. If the pasta sticks together it will not cook evenly and won't be very good. You'll be able to tell when you don't need to stir as often when you put your spoon in and don't feel pasta clumping together. The pasta box will tell you how long you'll need it to cook. Drain the pasta in the strainer in the sink. Shake the strainer so that all water drains out and put the pasta back in the pot. Mix with sauce and toppings as you see fit. Enjoy.

The "Bad-Ass Godfather" Super Bowl Subs

We have no shame in hanging up posters of Marlon Brando in Francis Ford Coppola's original "The Godfather" alongside Al Pacino in "Scarface" – we idolize them because they are bad to the bone, and we would like to claim at least some shared characteristics. In honor of our bad-ass movie icons, this sub will rock your world on Super Bowl Sunday or any day of the week... really. So in deciding between the Italian sub and a grilled Italian sausage sandwich, I couldn't decide so I combined to the two to create this bad-ass sub. Did I mention that caramelized onions are the secret to all sandwiches and have their way of injecting flavor without stealing the show? You don't even know they're there, so getting the caramelized onion thing (recipe follows) down is key. If you want to make the caramelized onions a few days before and cover and stick them in the fridge - that works too.

5 links sweet Italian sausage
5 links hot Italian sausage
4 tablespoons vegetable or extra-virgin olive oil
2 cups beef broth
1 teaspoon dried oregano*
1 teaspoon dried thyme*
1 teaspoon dried parsley*
(6) 6" sub rolls

If you don't have all three dried herbs, don't sweat it, you can add one, two or none, or substitute with dried basil.

Heat oil in a large skillet over medium heat. Pierce the sausage casings with a fork, then brown on all sides, about 5-8 minutes. Add beef broth, bring to a boil then cover and simmer on low heat for 10 minutes. Remove the sausages from the skillet, and park them in a bowl while you do the next step. SAVE the beef broth-don't throw it out because you can save it for dunking! Pour the broth into a bowl. Sprinkle the sausages with oregano, thyme, and parsley and stir until well-coated. Place links on a cutting board, then slice on the diagonal.

CARAMELIZED ONIONS & GREEN PEPPERS:

Heat butter and olive oil in a large skillet on medium heat, sauté onions first for 5 minutes then add the green peppers and continue sautéing until soft. Depending on how much you want to caramelize the onions it could be anywhere from 10-45 minutes! Salt and pepper throughout process to taste.

CARAMELIZED ONIONS & GREEN PEPPERS:
4 tablespoons butter
⅓ cup extra-virgin olive oil
2 chopped onions
2 thinly sliced green peppers
Salt and pepper to taste

Heat the rolls in the oven for 5 minutes at 350° and assemble subs, with little individual bowls for the beef broth (saved from earlier!) for dipping:

Sweet Italian sausage slices
Hot Italian sausage slices
Caramelized onions & green peppers
Chopped hot cherry peppers
Chopped banana peppers
Chopped pepperoncini
Dried chili peppers
Extra-virgin olive oil
Mayonnaise

Mustard
Pickles (sour or sweet)
Red wine vinegar
Shredded iceberg lettuce
Sliced ham
Sliced mozzarella or provolone (or both!)
Sliced salami
Sliced tomatoes

The subs are much easier to handle if they are cut in half on the diagonal.

Textbook Hero

1 large loaf Italian hero bread
½ pound thinly sliced deli ham, turkey or chicken or an assortment of all
½ pound favorite deli-sliced cheese - cheddar, Swiss, provolone or assortment of all
Hot sauce
handful bread & butter pickles or chips, drained or relish
Mayonnaise
Mustard
Salt and pepper
Aluminum foil

Preheat the oven to 350°. Slice the loaf horizontally with a serrated knife so you have a top and a bottom. Spread bottom half with mayonnaise, then salt and pepper, then arrange deli meat slices rolled up into balls, top with cheese slices, and spread the mustard on the top half of the loaf. Place the top half on and press down securely. Wrap in a sheet of foil then place in oven for 30 minutes. Remove from oven and place on a cutting board (keep the aluminum foil closed - don't open yet!) place a cinder block (or whatever weight you'd devised) on top and allowed to sit for 30 minutes (optional if you're too hungry to wait for this step...I've never been able to wait a whole 30 minutes when there is a hot sub sitting in front of me.)

Touchdown Roast Pork Hoagies

3-4 pound boneless pork shoulder *(or you can use the "bone in" pork shoulder but it will just be a little more work removing the pork from the bone once cooked)*
1 large ovenproof pot with lid
10 chopped garlic cloves
1 bottle dark beer or 2 cups red wine or dark rum
2 cups beef or vegetable broth *(you can make ahead with 2 cups boiling water and 2 beef bouillon cubes)*
1 teaspoon salt
1 teaspoon black pepper
2 large chopped onions
3 tablespoons extra-virgin olive or vegetable oil
Mustard
1 pound sliced cheese of your choice
8 hoagie rolls
Salt & pepper to taste

Preheat oven to 350°. Make little slits in the pork and insert the garlic cloves. Place the pork roast in the pot with the dark beer, vegetable broth, salt and pepper and cover. You may have to lower the shelf in your oven a notch or two for it to fit. While the roast is in the oven, heat 3 tablespoons oil in a heavy medium skillet, then sauté the onions until soft and light brown, stirring often. Roast for 3 hours or until the pork is very tender. Remove from oven. Take the pork roast and place it on a cutting board, saving the juice in the pot- this will be used for dipping! The pork should be able to be pulled apart easily or be sliced easily. Place the pork in a large serving bowl and ladle a little bit of the juices over it from the pot. Cover with foil to keep warm. Set out small individuals bowl so other College Men can serve themselves the broth for dipping. Heat the rolls in the oven for 5 minutes. Slather heated hoagie rolls with caramelized onions, mustard, cheese slices, and slices of roast pork then dip in the broth!

Waffle Burgers

MAKES 4 BURGERS

You can make hamburger taste like sausage with a few things from the pantry:

In a medium bowl, combine hamburger meat, onion, sugar, garlic powder, oregano, black pepper and chili flakes to the then mush it throughout the hamburger with your hands. Form 4 patties in the shape of slightly flattened tennis balls. Wash your hands with hot water and soap!!! Sprinkle a heavy skillet with 2 teaspoon salt (do not add any oil) then heat the skillet – make sure it is hot before adding the burgers or they will stick bigtime. Add patties, cover for 2 minutes then remove cover and press patties down with a spatula- if skillet is too dry add a few teaspoons of water. Flip the burgers then continue to cook pressing down again with a spatula a few more times to release the juices. This will take about 10-12 minutes. Make sure there is no rare meat when you cut into the burger. Toast frozen waffles and make your waffle burgers. Nuke maple syrup for a few seconds and pour over waffle burger.

1½ pounds hamburger meat
½ chopped onion
2 tablespoons light or dark brown sugar
2 teaspoons garlic powder (or chop up 5 cloves)
1 tablespoon dried oregano
1 teaspoon black pepper
1 tablespoon dried red chili pepper flakes
2 teaspoons salt
Maple Syrup
Condiments

Wasabi Burgers

MAKES 6 BURGERS

Lost your mojo? Whip up some wasabi burgers and get your mojo back!

WASABI MAYONNAISE:
In a small bowl, whisk together wasabi sauce, mayonnaise, orange juice, and orange zest. Cover and refrigerate.

PATTIES & BUNS:
In a large bowl, combine wasabi sauce, ground sirloin, ground chuck, toasted sesame oil, garlic, soy sauce, salt, black pepper and mix, using your hands, until well incorporated. Shape into 6 patties. Spray the grill rack while cold with vegetable oil then heat to medium. Grill burgers with lid closed, about 5 minutes per side. Spread wasabi mayo on toasted hamburger buns and eat!

WASABI MAYONNAISE:
3 tablespoons wasabi sauce (not wasabi paste)
1 cup mayonnaise
1 tablespoon orange juice
1 teaspoon orange zest

PATTIES & BUNS:
3 tablespoon prepared wasabi sauce (not wasabi paste)
1 pound ground sirloin (90% lean)
1 pound ground chuck
1 tablespoon toasted sesame oil
4 minced cloves garlic
2 teaspoons soy sauce
2 teaspoons salt
1 teaspoon freshly ground black pepper
Cooking spray for grill rack
6 hamburger buns, toasted just before serving

CHAPTER FIVE
Salads

There is no reason salad cannot have pizza in it and that's how my "Zesty Leftover Pizza Salad" came to be when I was trying to stretch out my leftovers. Based on what's in my fridge sometimes, I cook up my own version of the show "Chopped" which I have watched compulsively over the years. The premise is the chefs are given a basket of "mystery" ingredients and are expected to wow the judges with their ingenuity without having a meltdown. There are a few differences" I'm not being watched by millions and do not have a pantry and fridge with shelves of everything delicious to draw from, but I am the judge and I want whatever I'm making to taste really good if I'm going to make the effort. My salads are substantial and have everything from tons of fresh fruit to grilled pork chops - some are meals on their own. The salad dressing is key - there are some bottled salad dressings that are pretty good but nothing beats homemade dressings and all it takes, College Man, is a mini food processor (or a glass jar with a lid) and a few simple ingredients. My Aunt Mary taught me how to make the best dressing and it transforms a bowl of baby greens into the most delicious salad ever! Dressings don't have to be heavy, mayonnaise-based concoctions, although Thousand Island Dressing crushes it so it's right here on page 54.

BLT Salad

(1) 12-ounce package thick sliced bacon
1 head iceberg lettuce
½ cup mayonnaise
3 large, ripe tomatoes
2 cups sharp cheddar cheese, crumbled or shredded
Salt & pepper

DRESSING:
½ cup ketchup
½ cup mayonnaise

Slow cook bacon on medium-low heat until crisp in a large skillet, set onto paper towels and set aside. Wash iceberg lettuce, dry thoroughly with paper towels or salad spinner, then cut into 1" strips. Place the salad strips in a large salad bowl. Add dressing (make the dressing by combining the ketchup and mayonnaise in a small bowl) and toss until lettuce leaves are evenly coated. Chop tomatoes and arrange over iceberg lettuce. Sprinkle with cheddar cheese. Chop bacon and sprinkle over cheese. Salt and pepper to taste.

Farm Stand Tomato & Peach Salad with Peppery Pecans

3 ripe heirloom tomatoes
4 ripe peaches
8 ounces cottage cheese
½ pound candied pecans (see recipe below)
1/3 cup balsamic vinegar
1/3 cup extra-virgin olive oil

PEPPERY PECANS:
½ pound pecan halves
1 egg white
¾ cup sugar
1 teaspoon cayenne pepper
1 teaspoon cumin
1 teaspoon freshly ground black pepper
1 teaspoon salt

Road side farm stands always having sign reading "Tomatoes – Peaches" – although I remember specifically a place in rural Georgia that sold "Peches" so if you ever find those be sure to get as many as possible because they are very rare ;) – so I thought they should have a recipe with both it in!

TO MAKE CANDIED PECANS:
Preheat oven to 325°. In a small bowl, whisk egg white until slightly frothy, then add pecan halves and coat well. In a separate bowl, stir together sugar, cayenne, cumin, black pepper and salt. Fold egg white mixture into spice mixture then place on a lipped cookie sheet. Bake for 20-25 minutes, turning once after 15 minutes. Remove from oven, quickly scrape them off the baking sheet, transfer to a plate and allow to cool. If you don't do this they might be impossible to get off the baking sheet unless you have a jackhammer!

ASSEMBLY:
Slice tomatoes into ½" slices and arrange on the bottom of a flat serving dish, not a salad bowl. Cut peaches into ½" chunks and arrange over tomato slices. Dot with crumbled farmer's cheese. Salt lightly. Drizzle with balsamic vinegar and olive oil. Top with candied pecans.

Fruit Salad Platter Triple Dip

If you want to substitute or add other fruits like sliced kiwis, that'll work EXCEPT, bananas which will turn brown shortly after you cut them so don't cut them in advance. Rinse fruit then dry on paper towels, then arrange fruit on a platter. Now you can make the three dips: in a small bowl, combine peanut butter, brown sugar, and milk. Done! In another small bowl, combine yogurt and honey. Done! In a small pot, bring heavy cream just to a simmer, then whisk in chocolate, cinnamon, and chili powder until well melted. Remove from heat and allow to cool or you can serve it warm! Done!

½ pound cherries
½ pound red seedless grapes
½ pound green seedless grapes
½ pound strawberries
2 sliced green apples
2 sliced red apples

PEANUT BUTTER DIP:
½ cup smooth or chunky peanut butter
½ cup light or dark brown sugar
2 tablespoons milk or half and half

YOGURT DIP:
½ cup sour cream or Greek-style yogurt
½ cup honey or agave

CHOCOLATE DIP:
1 cup heavy cream
2 cups (a 10 – ounce bag) milk chocolate chips
½ teaspoon cinnamon
½ teaspoon chili powder

Greek Life Pasta Salad

(1) 1-pound box penne pasta (*you can substitute macaroni or other small pasta*)
1 cucumber, sliced lengthwise into 4 strips, then sliced into ¼" slices
1 red bell pepper, seeded and diced
2 chopped tomatoes
1 cup kalamata or black olives, pitted, and sliced in half
½ finely chopped red onion
8 ounces crumbled feta cheese
2 tablespoons minced parsley
2 minced garlic cloves
Juice of 1 lemon
1 tablespoon red wine vinegar
⅓ cup extra-virgin olive oil
Salt and pepper to taste

Cook pasta according to package directions and set aside to cool down - to keep it from sticking together, drizzle a little olive oil and stir it. When cooking pasta it's important to not just throw the pasta in the boiling water and then let it cook. You have to stir it every 30 seconds for the first few minutes to make sure that it doesn't stick together because if you do that then you'll just end up with a big block of carbs. Toss together all ingredients in large bowl. Cover and chill for later or serve at room temperature.

Green Salad & Aunt Mary's Dressing

SALAD:
1 large head romaine lettuce or Iceberg lettuce

DRESSING:
½ cup extra-virgin olive oil
3 finely diced garlic cloves
4 teaspoons Dijon-style mustard
Juice of 1 lemon
1 teaspoon salt

Cut off bottom of romaine lettuce, and tear off any tough or brown outer leaves and tips of leaves. Wash lettuce leaves in a salad spinner or rinse and lay out and dry on paper towels. The leaves need to be dry so the dressing will stick to them otherwise it just becomes a watery lettuce "soup"...tear or chop into bite-size pieces. To make the dressing, place all ingredients in a small blender for 1 minute or use a whisk to blend together in a medium bowl. Place lettuce in salad bowl, then toss with dressing just before serving.

Heirloom Tomato & Mozzarella Salad

Using the fresh mozzarella is key to this recipe (this usually comes wrapped in a ball in plastic wrap OR can be in plastic container with a little liquid which you can drain after opening)

Slice mozzarella cheese and tomatoes. Arrange on a platter, alternating with a thin slice of mozzarella and a slice of tomato. Sprinkle with chopped basil, then drizzle with olive oil, balsamic vinegar, salt and pepper. Cover and chill until ready to serve.

1 pound fresh mozzarella cheese
4 ripe heirloom tomatoes (or "ugly tomatoes")
Handful fresh basil leaves, chopped
⅓ cup extra-virgin olive oil
¼ cup balsamic vinegar

Salt & pepper to taste

Strawberry, Blueberry & Cherry Yogurt Salad

Combine all ingredients, in a bowl, stir gently and eat!

1 cup strawberries, sliced
1 cup blueberries
1 cup chopped cherries (pits removed)
2 cups Greek-style yogurt
2 tablespoons honey or agave

Thai Salad with Grilled Pork Chops

SALAD:
**1 large head chopped red leaf
 lettuce**
**1 large peeled and thinly
 sliced cucumber**
**1 large red bell pepper,
 cored, seeded, and sliced
 into thin strips**
**1 large yellow bell pepper,
 cored, seeded, and sliced
 into thin strips**
**1 bunch scallions, ends
 trimmed, sliced ¼" thick
 on diagonal**
**3 handfuls chow mein
 crunchy noodles**

SALAD DRESSING:
**½ cup smooth or crunchy
 peanut butter**
⅓ cup vegetable oil
Juice of 1 lemon
¼ cup soy sauce
1 teaspoon garlic powder
¼ cup water

PORK CHOPS:
8 thick boneless pork chops
3 minced garlic cloves
**1 tablespoon powdered
 ginger**
salt and pepper

SALAD DRESSING:
Whisk all ingredients together until smooth.

PORK CHOPS:
Marinate the pork chops in ½ cup of the dressing, minced garlic and powdered ginger in a bowl for 15 minutes while the grill is heating up. Grill chops 4-5 minutes per side. If there is no grill available or you're not in the mood to grill, heat a few tablespoons vegetable oil in a large, heavy skillet and pan fry the pork chops (you'll need to do this in 2 batches) then add then dressing, minced garlic and powdered ginger during the last 3 minutes of frying. Salt and pepper to taste.

TO SERVE:
Toss all salad ingredients together in large bowl and then add salad dressing and toss again. Place large mound of salad on each plate and top with grilled pork slices.

Thousand Island Dressing

½ cup mayonnaise
3 tablespoons ketchup
**1 tablespoon sweet
 pickle relish**

This is super versatile dressing that you can use on salads but also as a dipping sauce.

Stir together mayonnaise, catchup and sweet pickle relish. Cover and refrigerate.

Zesty "Leftover Pizza" Salad

Chop up lettuce and add to a large salad bowl. Warm up the pizza in the oven at 350° for 10 minutes so it's crispy. Just before serving, toss in all remaining ingredients, except lemon. Zest the lemon, sprinkle over salad, then cut lemon in half and squeeze juice over salad, removing any seeds.

1 head washed romaine lettuce
3 ripe tomatoes, cut into large chunks
¾ cup Aunt Mary's Caesar dressing (*see page 20*)
2 slices very crispy leftover pizza, cut into 1-inch cubes
¾ cup shaved Parmesan
1 tablespoon capers, drained
Salt and pepper to taste
Zest of 1 lemon
Juice of 1 lemon

TIDBITS AND TASTY THOUGHTS

Wash, *Then* Eat Your Veggies

There are so many recipes which don't require cooking vegetables and fruits. Between possible pesticides, herbicides and other chemicals and bacteria that fruits and vegetables are exposed to during transit and handling, taking the time to rinse them under running tap water before serving is key. There are also products on the market for washing produce. If something feels particularly waxy, like apples or cucumbers, add ½ cup apple cider vinegar to a bowl of water and let the produce sit for a few minutes to help remove that residue. Even organic produce may still need to be washed!

The Art of *Not* Following a Recipe

Some cooks follow the recipe to the letter - but what if they decide to break from the pack and, let's say, substitute an ingredient or two? This confidence comes after trying recipe after recipe and getting a handle on what's what. You've got to crawl before you walk, right? Or it stems from totally reckless behavior and creativity gone wild... A great pianist may play the works of others but eventually may feel inclined to compose his own symphony! The point of the story is it's ok to put your own twist on a recipe - one of exceptions may be that doing this when baking with a key ingredient like baking powder or baking soda in a cake might give it the texture of a brick - BUT forge ahead, and create your own recipes! Baking is more of a science than cooking, but what's the worst could happen? See "Recipes Gone Wrong" on page 20 ... or call somebody, anybody who knows more about cooking than you and ask them for their advice. They'll take it as a compliment when you appeal to their inner chef.

CHAPTER SIX

Side Dishes

Side dishes are meant to go with a main course and there is some thought to what is known as "pairing", but don't let the term intimidate you - it simply means which foods go with other foods. If you learn a few basics about pairing, then you'll feel more confident in the kitchen. For example, you wouldn't serve mashed potatoes, macaroni and cheese and potato salad with your fried chicken but geez, that does sound good...getting something green, as in vegetable, on the plate is good for a lot of reasons but look around and find green things to eat. My side dish recipes have lots of stick-to-the-College Man's-ribs potatoes, rice, beans, and noodles – your assignment is to go out and get something green like broccoli, spinach, or green beans – if you want to splurge, pick up some asparagus and trim off the lower tough stalks. No need to do anything fancy - steam them until tender in a pot with some water, then drain. Sprinkle with a little butter, lemon juice, salt and pepper and that does the trick.

Baked Potato Bar

MAKES 6

6 large russet potatoes or
   the biggest ones you have
   on hand
Sour cream
Butter
Fresh chopped chives
Fresh chopped green onions
Fresh chopped parsley
Chopped tomatoes
Chopped jalapenos
Any type shredded cheese
Salt & black pepper

Preheat oven to 400°. Wash potatoes, pierce with a fork in several places, then set directly on the rack in the oven. Bake for 45-50 minutes or until tender when pierced with a fork (if they are smaller potatoes, they will need less time in the oven). Cut in half, then serve with the fixings!

Baked "Sweetie Pie" Potatoes

SERVES 4

4 medium sweet potatoes
4 teaspoons butter
½ cup pecans or any nuts,
   chopped
Maple syrup

Preheat oven to 400°. Wash potatoes, then set sheet of aluminum foil directly on the rack in the oven to catch any drippings. Slit each potato with a small knife in two places so the steam can escape. Bake for 50-60 minutes or until tender when pierced with a fork. Cut in half, then serve with butter, pecans and heated maple syrup.

Chipotle Red Beans

SERVES 8 AS A SIDE DISH

(1) 16-ounce package dried
   red beans
Water
1 chopped onion
6 chopped garlic cloves
2 large chicken or vegetable
   bouillon cubes
1-2 teaspoons chipotle
   powder
Salt and black pepper
   to taste
8 cups hot, cooked rice

In a medium sauce pan, add black beans, then cover with enough water that it rises 6" above the beans. Stir in onion, garlic, bouillon cubes, chipotle powder, salt and pepper. Bring to a boil, cover, then lower heat and simmer, stirring occasionally. Keep covered and cook for 2 ½-3 hours, or until beans are soft. Check the liquid level and add more water if necessary. Ladle 1 cup beans into mini food processor and pulse or put in a bowl and smash with a fork. Stir the beans back into the pot and this will thicken up the beans. Serve over hot rice.

Collard Greens with Garlic & Parmesan Cheese

SERVES 6-8

Rinse the collard greens leaves, then trim off the thick stems at the base and cut out the tough spine in the middle of each leaf. Chop up or tear leaves into small pieces. Heat 3 tablespoons extra-virgin oil in a large skillet. Add garlic and sauté until translucent, about 2 minutes. Add water and chopped collard greens and sauté, covered, over low heat stirring occasionally for 10-15 minutes or until wilted. If there is excess liquid, uncover and continue to sauté. If not enough liquid, add a few more tablespoons water. Place in a serving bowl. Salt and pepper to taste. Sprinkle with parmesan cheese. Toss and serve.

2 heads collard greens
6 tablespoons extra-virgin olive
6 chopped cloves garlic
1½ cups water
Salt and pepper to taste
6 tablespoons freshly grated Parmesan cheese

Garlic Breath Garlic Bread

MAKES 2 LOAVES

And a reminder to be sure to serve this to your date because then you'll both have garlic breath and it won't matter... hopefully?

Preheat oven to 400°. Add softened butter (microwave for around 5-10 seconds if you just took it out of the fridge), chopped garlic and olive oil into a mini food processor and pulse until smooth, about 30 seconds or you can stir the ingredients together in a medium bowl. Using a serrated knife, cut into the loaves crosswise to make slices, but do not slice all the way through so the loaves stay intact. Take a spoon (easier than a knife) and spread the garlic butter equally in between each slice. I can promise you this - you will not get through this without eating at least one slice before it goes in the oven! Lay each loaf on a sheet of foil, making sure the foil extends beyond the ends of each loaf just in case any garlic butter melts, unless you like cleaning the oven...If you close the foil up around the loaves, they won't get nice and crusty on the top, so leave the foil open but bring it up around the edges so there's no drippage. Bake for 15 minutes or until lightly browned on top. Remove from oven, then place on cutting on board and cut all the way through the slices. This could be a meal in itself, College Man, but some nice red sauce would be nice to!

2 loaves bread (*baguette, Italian or any type you like*)
1 stick softened butter
4 cloves chopped garlic
1 teaspoon
½ cup extra-virgin olive oil

Aluminum foil

59

Noodles with Peanut Sauce

SERVES 4-6

1 pound spaghetti or thin linguine, cooked and drained

2 seeded and thinly sliced red bell peppers

6 scallions, white and green parts, into ¼" pieces

DRESSING:

½ cup vegetable oil

½ cup rice vinegar

½ cup soy sauce *(or about 20 of those little packets you saved from your last Chinese food order)*

2 tablespoons honey

2 large garlic cloves, finely minced or grated

2 teaspoons ginger powder

4 tablespoons white or black sesame seeds, or a combination

¾ cup smooth or crunchy peanut butter

6 tablespoons minced parsley *(or cilantro leaves)*

DRESSING (MAKES ABOUT 2 CUPS):

Cook spaghetti according to package directions then transfer to a large serving bowl with red peppers and scallions. Whisk together all dressing ingredients or pulse in a food processor. Transfer spaghetti to a serving bowl, then pour dressing over spaghetti and toss until well coated. Garnish with parsley. Serve hot or cold.

Orange Rice

SERVES 6-8

2 cups uncooked rice

3 ¾ cups water

1 teaspoon salt

Juice of 1 orange

Zest the orange

The color of the rice is not a bright orange, but the flavor is!

In a medium sauce pan, add rice, water, salt, orange juice and zest. Bring to a boil, then simmer, covered, for 20 minutes. Turn off heat, and keep covered, but let it remain on the hot burner for 5 minutes. If the rice appears undercooked, add a few teaspoons water (do not stir), then cover and allow to sit 10 more minutes. Fluff with a fork before serving. You can remedy undercooked rice, but you can't remedy overcooked rice!

Oven Roasted Potato Wedges

SERVES 4-6

Preheat oven to 450°. Place a lipped cookie sheet or large metal pan in oven for 5 minutes to heat up. Meanwhile, peel potatoes, rinse, dry and cut each potato lengthwise into 10-12 wedges. In a large bowl, gently toss potato wedges with all ingredients. Arrange on heated lipped cookie sheet so they are not overlapping, and bake for 30 minutes, turn using a metal spatula (you really have to scrape them off using some force), then continue baking another 15 minutes, or until ready. Scrape the fries loose from the baking sheet with a spatula at an angle to get *underneath the fries,* or they may end up sticking. Once you have loosened them, you can leave them on the baking sheet to stay warm. Salt to taste. Serve with ketchup horseradish mayonnaise or Yummy Sauce (see recipe on page 70)

6 Russet or Yukon Gold potatoes
4 tablespoons extra-virgin olive or vegetable oil
1 teaspoon salt + salt to taste
1 teaspoon black pepper
1 teaspoon paprika, cayenne or chipotle powder
1 teaspoon garlic salt

DIPPING SAUCE:
½ cup ketchup
½ cup mayonnaise
¼ cup prepared horseradish*

***sold refrigerated in small jars in supermarkets**

Pirate Baked Beans

SERVES 6 AS A SIDE DISH

In a large heavy skillet, fry up bacon. Place bacon on a paper towel and reserve drippings in the skillet. Immediately eat one of the strips of bacon because you know you want to. Sauté onions in bacon drippings until soft. Add beans, ketchup, brown sugar, rum, apple juice, chipotle peppers, molasses, mustard, black pepper and stir together well. Bring to a boil and simmer for 8-10 minutes, stirring often. Preheat oven to 325°. Transfer beans into an 8" x 8" lightly greased baking dish. Chop the reserved bacon and sprinkle over beans. Bake, covered, for 1½ hours, stirring occasionally. Allow to sit for a few minutes to thicken before serving.

6 slices thick-cut bacon
(2) 15-ounce cans unsalted navy beans (*about 3 ½ cups, do not drain*)
1 medium red onion, finely chopped
1 cup ketchup
¾ cup light or dark brown sugar
½ cup rum
1 cup apple juice
⅓ cup chipotle peppers in adobo sauce, seeds removed through a sieve (*OK to substitute powdered chipotle*)
1 tablespoon molasses
2 tablespoons Dijon mustard
Freshly ground black pepper to taste

Yukon Gold Mashed Potatoes

SERVES 4

6 medium Yukon gold potatoes (or whichever potatoes you have on hand)
½ -¾ cup milk or half and half
4 tablespoons butter
½ teaspoon salt
½ teaspoon black pepper

Peel and cut each potato into eight pieces. Place in medium pot filled with cold water. Bring to a boil, then simmer, uncovered, about 20 minutes or until tender. Drain then return the hot pot to stove top and lower the heat. Add milk, butter, salt and pepper then remove from burner. Mash with a fork or potato masher to the desired consistency. If too thick, add a few teaspoons more milk. Salt and pepper to taste.

Notes:

_____

_____

_____

_____

_____

_____

_____

_____

_____

_____

The Nose Test for Fish

What to look for when buying fish? A quick "nose test" will let you know of the fish is fresh. If it as any hint of an unappealing odor, throw it away. Cooking it will not help the situation. Fresh fish should not smell or taste fishy and tuna fish out of the can tastes nothing like actual tuna fish, in fact, not remotely any similarity between the two – it's just the way it's processed and canned that makes the difference. And when you do buy tuna in the can, buy the white albacore in water, not the chunk tuna in oil or water which sorta looks like cat food...the art of cooking fish is to be sure to not overcook it, because within a quick moment, it can be rubbery and dry, so multi-tasking is not advisable. You, College Man, cannot be jamming to Phish while cooking your fish or it will not go over well.

When It Comes to Buying Wine...

There's nothing more appealing than a College Man who knows how to select a great bottle of wine - the one thing that is limiting is the budget but there are good wines for not a wad of cash. How much wine do you need? A bottle of wine serves 4-5 people who are drinking like old people so your bottle will probably serve more like 2-3. You're on a budget but there are good wines for less than $10 a bottle. Even sparkling wines like Champagne and prosecco can be found on the cheap! Go to your local wine shop and ask questions - consider it a wine library. A knowledgeable staff is always happy to help in steering you in the right direction because ultimately the shop wants you to become a customer on a regular basis. Be adventurous and buy a few varietals you're unfamiliar with - for example, grab what you're familiar with like Chardonnay and Merlot but try Pinot Blanc, Grenache, Tempranillo, Gewürztraminer or Shiraz. This also allows you to taste different wines to determine what you really enjoy. Once you learn more about wines, you won't break out in hives when trying to impress a date. There are also great apps that allow the user to take a photo of the label of the wine and provides average prices, ratings and reviews and food pairings.

Leftovers

So let's say you're at a tailgating party and food is set out for a few hours but you have some leftovers? IF the food has been kept cold during the festivities (like potato salad or coleslaw for example), then it would be OK to cover and refrigerate the leftovers. But if the potato salad has been sitting out on a warm or hot day and is not sitting on a bed of ice, you need to DITCH IT. This is the thing - bacteria can keep growing in the fridge. It doesn't just magically stop once you stick it in the fridge. If some food in your fridge has green or white stuff growing on it (unless it's blue cheese) DITCH IT. If it smells bad, DITCH IT. If you taste something and it "fizzes" or is tangy (like sour cream or yogurt), DITCH IT. If there is something MOVING on its own, then it is beyond your ability to handle the situation - call a HAZMAT hotline immediately.

Mancave

Our sofa was its own living, breathing animal and I'm not even talking about the bacteria! In its heyday, the sofa must have looked enticing on a showroom floor somewhere teasing a buyer with its manly dark brown "pleather" (plastic leather), billowing cushions and hefty armrests. It was on the low side to begin with, but when you actually sat down on it, it enveloped you to the point where you were practically sitting on the floor with a thin barrier of pleather between you. Getting back out required an engine hoist and a few helpers. We watched the game in the sofa, since it was impossible to sit "on" the sofa. It was super cozy, except for the parts covered in duct tape which were just plain tacky, but we didn't care. Hundreds of dollars' worth of coins made their way in between the cushions, never to be retrieved. We won't even get into the "love sack" that was in our living room, as well.

CHAPTER SEVEN

Main Courses

Admit it - you're in a circle of trust, College Man - it's OK to feel homesick! These recipes can take the edge off - comfort food, as any Psychology Major will tell you, can make you feel better emotionally and in a whole host of other ways. There's something about a pot of simmering chili that reminds us of the good old days at home when piping hot meals magically appeared on our dinner table - the magician was that parent or somebody who loved you enough to make it for you. Now it's time to step up and make your own pot of chili - the two secret ingredients that make the chili stand out? Dark beer and cumin - these will work that magic we mentioned above. Clear your schedule - making a super delicious chili will only take an hour of your life. And please don't say that you don't have time - it's obnoxious but true - you have to MAKE time. Making the "I'm Homesick Pot Roast" recipe will be like babysitting your little cousin for 3 hours - you can't leave the house but you don't have to check in on it every single minute.

For you fans of hot 'n spicy, rum and shrimp come together with some red curry and explode with flavors over rice or straight out of the pot if you forgot to buy rice. Rice will not magically appear if you forgot to throw it in the grocery cart...

Broc 'n Mac 'n Cheese

1 pound macaroni
1 head broccoli

SAUCE:
4 tablespoons flour
4 tablespoons butter
2 cups hot milk
2 cups shredded cheddar
cheese
1 teaspoon salt
1 teaspoon black pepper

Cook the macaroni according to package directions. While the macaroni boils, prepare the broccoli by either steaming it or boiling, covered, it in a pot with 2" of water. Drain broccoli and set aside to cool. Cut off the thick stem and then chop into 1" pieces. In a medium skillet, heat butter on medium heat, then whisk in flour. The butter will immediately begin to absorb the flour and it will quickly thicken into a pasty consistency. Keep whisking for 1 minute, then whisk in hot milk. Continue whisking until it mixture is smooth and begins to bubble, about 1½– 2 minutes. Stir in 1 cup cheddar cheese during the last minute of cooking or until it melts, whisking constantly. If sauce needs to be thinned out, whisk in a few tablespoons milk. Salt and pepper to taste. Preheat oven to 350°. Transfer the cooked macaroni into a large buttered baking dish. Stir in cooked broccoli and sauce then sprinkle with remaining cup of cheddar cheese. Bake for 15 minutes or until cheese melts.

Chicken Enchiladas

2 tablespoons vegetable oil
2 pounds boneless chicken
breasts
1 teaspoon adobo
seasoning (can be found in
international section)
½ teaspoon ground cumin
1 small diced yellow onion
1 large minced garlic clove
½ diced green bell pepper
2 peeled and diced carrots
6 diced plum tomatoes
(1) 7-ounce can chopped
green chilies
1 package 8" flour tortillas
(10 in a pack)
(2) 10-ounce cans enchilada
sauce
16 ounces grated Colby Jack
cheese
Shredded lettuce
1 cup sour cream

Preheat oven to 350°. Sprinkle adobo and cumin over chicken. Heat oil in large skillet over medium heat. Add chicken and cook 6 minutes a side – flipping every 2 minutes or so. The cook time will change depending on how big the chicken breasts are – a good indication that the chicken is done is when the liquid is clear when you press on it and juices come out. Transfer to plate. Add onion, garlic, green peppers, and carrots to skillet, and sauté for 8 minutes or until softened. Add diced tomatoes and chilies and cook for 3 more minutes. Meanwhile, cut chicken into ¼" slices. Add chicken to skillet and mix to combine. Simmer for 2 more minutes. Pour 1 can enchilada sauce into large baking pan. Divide chicken mixture evenly into each tortilla and fold to close, adding enchiladas (seam down) to the pan. Pour remaining enchilada sauce evenly over tops. Sprinkle with grated cheese. Bake for 20 minutes. Serve with shredded lettuce and sour cream.

In a large pot, heat oil then sauté onions and garlic until soft. Add ground beef, then stir and break apart with a spoon or spatula until browned. Drain any excess fat if necessary. Add all remaining ingredients and bring to a simmer. Cover and continue to simmer on low heat for 1 hour, stirring occasionally. Serve with toppings.

Chili That Bites Back!

1 tablespoon vegetable oil
2 diced onions
4 chopped cloves garlic
4 medium cans kidney beans
2 pounds lean ground beef
1 bottle dark beer or 1-2 cups red wine
4 tablespoons chili powder
1 tablespoon cumin
2 large cans chopped tomatoes (include the liquid!)
Salt to taste

TOPPINGS:
Shredded cheese
Green onions, chopped
½ pound cooked and chopped crispy bacon
Sour cream
Corn bread, crumbled

In a heavy large pot, heat oil then sauté onions until translucent, stirring often. Add chuck roast to the pot with the onions, then brown roast on all sides, about 4 minutes per side. Add carrots, mushrooms, beef broth, wine, brown sugar, salt and pepper. Bring to a boil, then simmer on low heat, covered, for 2 ½ – 3 hours or until tender. Check every half hour to make sure the liquid level is not too low. Add a little water or more beef broth if needed. Salt and pepper to taste. Serve over rice or mashed potatoes (see previous recipes).

"I'm Homesick" Pot Roast

3-3½ pound boneless beef chuck roast (remember to do the "nose" test!)
3 tablespoons vegetable oil
1 medium chopped onion
3 peeled and coarsely chopped carrots
(1) 1-pound package white button mushrooms, sliced*
***if you decide to skip the mushrooms, then you need to add ½ cup water as a substitute, since they provide a lot of liquid when they cook**
4 cups beef broth
1 cup red wine
½ cup light or dark brown sugar
1 teaspoon salt
1 teaspoon black pepper

Knockout Meat Balls in Killer Sauce

SERVES 6-8 (MAKE APPROXIMATELY 65 MEATBALLS)

3 pounds ground beef
6 slices white bread
1 cup milk
2 beaten eggs
1 finely chopped onion
1 teaspoon salt
1 teaspoon black pepper

SAUCE:
1 large chopped onion
⅓ cup Worcestershire sauce
1 cup white vinegar
¾ cup sugar
2 ¼ cups ketchup
2 ¼ cups water

Chop bread and soak in milk in a medium bowl. In another medium bowl, combine ground beef, eggs, chopped onion, salt and pepper. Add the bread-soaked milk and mix well. You do this by really getting in there using your hands, making sure the ingredients are well incorporated (like don't leave a bunch of egg and raw onions at the bottom of the bowl!). Shape the meat into balls, about the size of a ping pong ball. Why you would have the size of a ping pong ball imprinted in your brain? Mindless hours spent playing beer pong could have something to do with it, unless you go to school in a "dry" county, which means you spend a lot of time in the neighboring "wet" county. Make sure you scrub your hands and get rid of any raw meat anywhere that you dropped on the counter! Preheat oven to 350°. Arrange meatballs in a baking dish (you will have to bake them in two batches). Bake meatballs on the middle rack in the oven for 45-50 minutes. Now, make the sauce: You have to use a large pot because the meatballs are going to end up in it once they come out of the oven. Stir together onion, Worcestershire sauce, vinegar, sugar, ketchup and water, and bring to a simmer. Remove the meatballs from the oven and drain the liquid from the meatballs. Transfer them to the large pot on the stove where you have the sauce. Cover and simmer for 30 minutes on low heat. Serve over mashed potatoes, pasta, or rice or on their own, they are KILLER!

Red & White Bean Smokin' Turkey Chili

SERVES 6-8

2 tablespoons extra-virgin olive oil
1 pound ground turkey, white meat
1 pound ground turkey, dark meat
1 large finely chopped onion
2 tablespoons chili powder
(4) 15-ounce cans red kidney beans, drained and rinsed
(4) 15-ounce cans Great Northern white beans, drained and rinsed
1 small can tomato paste
(1) 7-ounce can chipotle peppers in adobo sauce (remove seeds and any stems, then chopped)
2 bottles dark beer
1 cup water
Salt and pepper to taste

Heat olive oil in heavy stock pot, about 1 minute, then sauté onions until translucent. In a separate heavy skillet, brown ground turkey. Drain any excess liquid. Add ground turkey to the onions, and add all remaining ingredients. Bring to a boil then simmer, covered, for 25-30 minutes, stirring occasionally. Serve hot with shredded cheese, sour cream, chopped green onions and crusty bread.

Spicy Chinese Veggies Stir-Fry

Cook your rice while you're making this so it will ready by the time you're finished. Heat coconut oil in a heavy skillet over medium heat. Add ginger powder and chili powder and stir for 1 minute. Stir in garlic and onions. Sauté for 2-3 minutes, adding a bit more coconut oil if too dry. Stir in carrots, cabbage, bell pepper, stirring constantly for about 6-8 minutes. Lower heat then add soy sauce and vinegar. Stir to coat the vegetables well and continue stirring and simmering for 2-3 more minutes. Serve over hot rice.

4-6 cups hot rice, cooked according to package directions
2 tablespoons coconut or vegetable oil (or more as needed)
1 tablespoon ginger powder
2 tablespoons crushed red pepper flakes
5 minced garlic cloves
½ chopped medium red onion
2 carrots, peeled and cut into thin strips
2 cups shredded purple cabbage
2 red or green bell peppers, seeds removed & cut into small strips
4 tablespoons soy sauce (did you save those little packets the last time you broke down and ordered Chinese? Look under your sofa...)
2 tablespoons rice wine vinegar (optional – if you don't have it, no biggie)

Spicy Rum Shrimp

In a medium bowl, combine rum, red onion, garlic, curry paste, chili powder, salt and pepper. Add shrimp and coat with mixture. In a large heavy skillet, heat coconut oil, then add shrimp, cooking on each side, until shrimp turns a light pink. Serve over hot rice and sprinkle with parsley.

¼ cup dark or spiced rum
1 medium red onion, chopped
5 garlic cloves, chopped
1 teaspoon red curry paste
2 tablespoons red chili powder or chili pepper flakes
½ teaspoon salt
½ teaspoon freshly ground black pepper
2 pounds medium shrimp, peeled and deveined
2 tablespoons coconut oil
6 cups hot cooked rice
Parsley, finely chopped (for garnish)

Teriyaki Chicken, Beef & Rice Stir-Fry with Yummy Sauce

1 pound boneless chicken breasts
1 pound sirloin steak tips
6 eggs, scrambled
3 tablespoons vegetable oil
6 cups hot rice*, cooked according to package directions
(*if you want to buy 3 bags of microwavable teriyaki rice, that's an option)
¾ cup teriyaki sauce
Yummy sauce

TERIYAKI SAUCE:
¼ cup water
⅓ cup soy sauce
1 teaspoon ginger powder
2 tablespoons light or dark brown sugar
3 tablespoons rice wine vinegar
⅓ cup sugar
4 cloves minced garlic (use your mini food processor if you want to get it really fine)
1 tablespoon corn starch* mixed with 2 tablespoons water

YUMMY SAUCE:
1 teaspoon tomato paste (or substitute 2 teaspoons ketchup)
¼ stick melted butter
1 teaspoon garlic powder
1 cup mayonnaise
1 teaspoon sugar
3 tablespoons water
½ teaspoon cayenne pepper (optional)

Once you have made your hot rice, make the Teriyaki Sauce (recipe follows) and decide how much you want to use, about half of it or all of it depending on your taste, and save the rest for another time. It will keep in the fridge for 2 weeks. Heat oil in a large skillet, then brown the chicken and steak, transfer to a cutting board. Cut chicken and steak into bite-size pieces-it's easier to cut the meat when it's cooked than when it is raw. Heat a little butter and scramble the eggs in another medium skillet. Add the rice and teriyaki sauce, chicken and steak pieces, and cooked scrambled eggs into the large skillet. Serve hot and drizzle with Yummy Sauce (recipe follows).

TERIYAKI SAUCE: MAKES ABOUT ¾ CUP
*This helps to thicken the Teriyaki Sauce but if you don't have it on hand, don't worry about it. It just means your teriyaki sauce will be a bit thinner but will still taste great!

Assemble all ingredients in a glass bowl, then stir. Nuke for 4 minutes.

YUMMY SAUCE: MAKES ABOUT 1½ CUPS
Add all ingredients in your mini-food processor and pulse, about 1 minute or until smooth. Cover and keep refrigerated until ready to use.

SERVES 3-4

Zesty Lemon Chicken

Preheat oven to 400°. Leave the skin on the chicken, but cut off excess fatty skin from the breasts using kitchen scissors (or any kind of scissors but wash and dry them well afterwards). Rinse with cold water, pat dry with paper towels. Squeeze juice from lemons and remove seeds. Place chicken in a baking dish, then pour wine around the edges of the chicken, sprinkle chopped garlic in wine, drizzle with lemon juice. Rub the butter over the skin (yes, with your fingers and then wash your hands), then salt and pepper chicken. Roast for 30-45 minutes, or until the skin starts to turn a light golden brown, carefully pulling it out to baste it once in the juices using a spoon. No need to turn the chicken while cooking.

3 chicken breasts (about 3 pounds), on the bone with skin
1 cup white wine, or 1 bottle (or can) beer
6 chopped garlic cloves
4 lemons
2 tablespoons butter
Salt and pepper

TIDBITS AND TASTY THOUGHTS

Save the Bacon Fat!

There are many worthwhile campaigns - save the whales, save the polar ice caps and save the planet - but even almost as important is the save the bacon fat campaign! After you finish frying your bacon, allow the bacon fat to cool and store into a glass jar or plastic sealable container in the fridge. It will firm up and turn white – don't worry, when it is heated it turns clear again. Bacon fat can be added to practically anything instead of oil or butter and it will add a mild hint of bacon flavor, but certainly not overwhelm the core flavors of any recipe. If you've cooked dinner and find it's tasting a little on the bland side, just stir in a tablespoon of bacon fat and it brings out all the flavors - hamburgers, steak, potatoes, and rice will benefit from a little bacon fat. Even when baking, a little bacon fat instead of oil or shortening work miracles!

Leftovers Makeover

When you're that hungry you're really not caring how good it is and you're thrilled that there's something to chow down on but the word 'leftovers' has such a negative connotation - of course nobody wants leftovers! 'Left' as in 'abandoned' and 'overs' as in well... 'overs'.

Time to come up with a new name for leftovers and here is one suggestion: 'Spaghetti reboot' (of course that only applies if you're having spaghetti, but 'reboot' and 'spaghetti' sounded so good together. College Man, believe me, there is magic in leftovers (it sounded good at the time.) A leftover baked potato, looking shriveled and rubbery in its brown skin, can come to life again once peeled, sprinkled with capers, olive oil, and salt and pepper. Topped with a poached egg sprinkled with fresh parsley, it stands on its own, making a comeback like Brittany Spears and her epic comeback after her 2000's meltdown (she looks good now - check it out)! Rice can spring back to life when placed in a bowl, to which steaming vegetable or chicken broth has been added, sprinkled with sliced green onions and red chili pepper flakes – a new meal is born. How to store leftovers? Transfer leftovers to an airtight container and refrigerate – I think you can handle that, pretty straightforward, College Man. Making sure the leftovers are properly refrigerated is key to food safety. Most leftovers should be eaten with 2-3 days, or fewer if highly perishable. Sometimes a dish tastes even better the second day when the flavors have had time to meld, unless of course it's a sandwich, then it's probably a soggy mess and you need to have eaten it yesterday...

CHAPTER EIGHT

Late Night Snacks

Let's face it, it comes down to what state you're in and how much effort you want to make when it comes to your midnight snack. If you're up late studying, taking a short break to prepare something tasty might be just what you need. But if you're stumbling in the door having partied too much but coherent enough to be hungry, the last thing you want to do is make something with more than one ingredient. In that state, and I'm speaking from experience, a bag of chips or mysterious leftovers, eaten cold, serve the purpose. You won't remember the next morning anyway. We seriously love cheese (from caseus for you Latin Majors) so you'll find it in many of this chapter's recipes - from quick and easy Cheesy Nachos and Popcorn Parmigiana to Beer and Cheese Fondue and Pizza Bread. When it comes to buying cheese, look around for one you've never tried before and give it a try. There's a whole world of cheese out there and knowing a little about cheese, like anything, comes in handy. Throwing around some impressive cheese knowledge will impress your roommate's parents and you may even redeem yourself in their eyes - to this day you feel bad about "the dart incident". Anyway, where there's salty, there's gotta be sweet so that's where the Grilled PB & J comes in - with a glass of cold milk, College Man.

Beer & Cheese Fondue

½ stick melted butter
¼ cup flour
2 ½ cups shredded sharp
   cheddar cheese
1 cup Guinness or dark beer
1 teaspoon Tabasco Sauce or
   to taste
2 chopped dill pickles
½ teaspoon black pepper
Thick slices of toasted bread

No need for a fondue pot or any fancy equipment!

In a microwave safe bowl, whisk together butter and flour. Nuke for 1 minute then remove and whisk mixture. Nuke for 30 more seconds then whisk in cheese, beer, Tabasco, chopped dill pickles and black pepper. Nuke for 2 more minutes, remove and whisk again until smooth. Dig in with pieces of toasted bread!

Boiled Peanuts in Old Bay

5 pounds "green" peanuts
   in the shell *("green" in this
   sense means "raw")*
20 cups water
1 cup salt
6-8 tablespoons Old Bay
   Seasoning

Rinse the peanuts in a large colander. Put the peanuts, water, salt and Old Bay seasoning in a large pot. Bring to a boil, then turn the heat down to a simmer, cover, and simmer for 3 hours or all day – it depends on how you like your peanut shells. Check water level frequently and add more water as needed. The more time the peanuts cook, the softer the shells will be. Let's state the not-so-obvious: you do NOT eat the shells. You would normally throw the peanuts shells on the ground after eating the peanuts outside but if you're inside, keep a trash can and practice your hook shot... KAREEM!

Grilled Peanut Butter & Jelly

MAKES 4

8 slices bread
Peanut butter
Jelly, any kind you like
Soft butter *(nuke it for a few
   seconds in a bowl)*

Spread 4 slices of bread with peanut butter. Spread the remaining 4 slices with jelly. Slap them together. Here is the *secret to successful grilled* PB & Js. Take soft butter and spread it on *both sides of the outside of the sandwiches.* If you have a panini grill, you're in luck and you know how to use it! If not, take a skillet, put some butter in it until it begins to bubble, making sure the butter does not turn brown. Place as many sandwiches in without overcrowding, and press down gently with a spatula. You can peek at the underside to see if they are turning golden brown. If yes, turn over the sandwiches, add a little more butter to the pan if too dry. Press down gently on the sandwiches a few times as they grill. You can use the same technique of buttering the outside of the sandwich even when you're using the panini grill, too.

Magic Cheesy Pretzel Sticks

SERVES 4-6

Preheat oven to broil. Spray an 8" x 8" glass baking pan with cooking spray or oil lightly (so the cheese doesn't stick). Arrange the pretzel sticks side by side. You can use metal but it will be a little harder to get the melted cheese out of the corners. Lay the cheese slices and chopped jalapeños over half of the pretzel sticks so you will be able to pick up the pretzel from the bottom part. Broil for 1 to 1 ½ minutes – don't walk away, College Man, or you will be setting off your smoke alarm... Remove from oven and dig in! And turn off the broiler! I may or may not have been doing a little bit more than just drinking while I came up with this recipe... don't knock it till you've tried it.

15 large pretzel sticks
8 slices deli cheese or any type
15 chopped jalapeño slices from the jar, drained

Midnight Cheesy Nachos

SERVES 4

Preheat oven to 350°. Spread out tortilla chips in large baking pan (with edges).

Spread beans over tortilla chips. Sprinkle cheddar cheese over beans. Place in oven until cheese is well melted, approximately 10 minutes. Top with salsa and sour cream. Serve hot!

1 large bag tortilla chips
2 medium cans pinto, pink, kidney or black beans, drained
2 cups shredded cheddar cheese
1 cup tomato salsa
1 cup sour cream

Nutella Marshmallow Treats

MAKES 38-42 TREATS

(A reminder to watch out for those who have nut allergies! They may be allergic to hazelnuts!)

In a heavy, large skillet, melt ¾ stick butter over low heat, then stir in marshmallows and Nutella until melted. Turn off the heat (but keep the skillet on the burner) then stir in the rice cereal until well coated with the mixture. In a small bowl, nuke ¼ stick butter, then pinch off pieces of the mixture, dip it half way in the butter and roll into 1" balls. If the mixture gets stuck to your hands, butter your hands. Arrange on a buttered serving plate.

¾ stick butter + ¼ stick butter
1 package miniature marshmallows
4 tablespoons Nutella or other brand hazelnut and chocolate spread
4 cups rice cereal (like Rice Crispies)

Open Faced Broiled Cheese

MAKES 6 SANDWICHES

Preheat the broiler to high. Lay out the bread on a cookie sheet, top with cheese. Watch them in the broiler so they don't burn! It doesn't get any easier than this, College Man. Just don't fall asleep or pass out (from fatigue of course) with the broiler on. DON'T FORGET TO TURN IT OFF!

6 slices bread
12 slices cheese

Pizza Bread

SERVES 4

8 slices thick bread
¼ cup extra-virgin olive oil
3 cloves finely chopped garlic *(or 1 tablespoon garlic salt or powder)*
1 tablespoon capers, drained
2 medium chopped tomatoes, seeds discarded
½ cup kalamata chopped olives *(or your favorite olives)*
1 cup shredded mozzarella or whichever cheese is on hand
Black pepper

Preheat oven to 350°. Arrange sliced bread on a lipped baking pan. Sprinkle with olive oil, then top with garlic, capers, tomatoes, olives, remaining olive oil, cheese, and black pepper. Place on middle rack of oven. Bake for 10-15 minutes.

Popcorn Parmigiano

MAKES 10-12 CUPS

1 cup popcorn kernels
½ stick melted butter
1 tablespoon garlic powder
1 teaspoon salt
½ teaspoon black pepper
½ cup grated Parmesan cheese

For $20-$25, make one of the best investments you'll ever make – pick up a hot air popcorn popper or ask a relative for it as a gift. No oil needed, just popcorn kernels (which are cheap) and no oily pots to clean up. This is when the fun part starts: (see directions on how to make popcorn in a pot below*)

Pop the corn kernels in the hot air popper. Nuke the butter until melted, then drizzle over popcorn. Sprinkle with garlic powder, salt, black pepper and Parmesan cheese and a few drops olive oil. Mangia!

*If using a pot, use a medium-size pot that has a thick bottom, because otherwise it will burn quickly and there's nothing more vile-tasting than burned popcorn. Heat 4 tablespoons extra-virgin olive oil over medium-high heat, then toss in a few kernels, stand back and take cover, then wait until they pop. This is your signal to add the rest of the kernels, then shake the pot gently side to side a few times so the kernels lay flat in the bottom and they become coated in oil. Place the lid on top (the best type would be a clear lid to keep an eye on your progress, but not essential). After a minute or two, the kernels will all start to pop. Shake the pot from side to side and back and forth over the burner every few seconds as the popping continues. The time will vary but it should take about 5-6 minutes – great workout for the forearms. When you hear just a few pops, remove from the burner and transfer into a serving bowl right away. Don't worry, you popped it just right–but there will be some unpopped kernels left at the bottom of the pot. (Don't reuse them.)

Quesadillas in a Mad Skillet

MAKES 2 QUESADILLAS

In a skillet large enough to accommodate a tortilla, heat 1 teaspoon olive oil over medium-low heat. Add a tortilla to the skillet then sprinkle with 1 cup cheese and chopped jalapeño. If you want to add cooked chicken, do it now. Top with another tortilla and press it down gently with a spatula. When the underside begins to turn light brown and the cheese begins to melt (about 1 minute), flip it over and allow the cheese to continue melting and the tortilla to brown on the underside. If you flip it too early, it will fall apart and a botched quesadilla is not representative of your newfound culinary talents. Another thing- if you get over zealous with the amount of ingredients you put in the quesadilla, it will get too soggy, so remember that less is more. Cut into quarters with pizza cutter or sharp knife, and serve with sour cream, salsa, and hot sauce.

- 4 teaspoons olive or vegetable oil
- (4) 8" flour tortillas
- 4 cups shredded Monterey Jack cheese or any combination of cheese
- 2 tablespoons chopped jalapeños *(from a can or a jar ok)*
- 1 cup chopped, cooked chicken, steak or ham
- ½ cup sour cream
- ½ cup salsa
- Hot sauce

TIDBITS AND TASTY THOUGHTS

The Power of Brownies

If you want to smooth out practically anything with the roommates, celebrate a great semester, a team's win (or console a team's loss), or an overdue break-up, nothing goes further than the Power of Brownies! Buy 2 boxes of brownie mix, make them, cut them into squares and place them on a platter and watch the transformation begin! With tears brimming in their eyes, those who are munching on these brownies forget their issues, all animosity melts away, and all wounds are healed within 30 seconds or however long it takes to scarf down a brownie...try it!

Kitchen Fires

Yes, kitchen fires do happen! First and foremost -stay calm. Sure, that's all good in theory, but panic is more likely to take over, so move quickly and be smart... After hot sauce and a bottle opener, the most important thing to have in the kitchen is a fire extinguisher. Check out that dusty fire extinguisher that's been hanging there before you were born. It has now become dusty, red "art". Check the gauge and if it's questionable, get a new one – they are not expensive and could save your butt, no joke. This is the thing – you have other options if your fire extinguisher is whack or if you can't find one! If your oven or microwave catches fire, close the doors! BUT, if the oven continues to smoke, CALL THE FIRE DEPARTMENT. This is where the science part comes in –if there is no oxygen to feed the fire, the fire goes out. If you have an oil or grease fire in your frying pan, water can sometimes be the worst thing to extinguish it. Grab a lid and cover the flames, then remove the lid and the pan from the burner and turn off the burner. If you don't have a lid, you can throw baking soda or salt on it to extinguish the fire. Water doesn't work well on oil or grease fires, and it can make things worse by spreading the fire if the grease splatters out of the pan! NEVER be embarrassed to call the Fire Department. Start by getting a good fire extinguisher or by dating a fire eater!

CHAPTER NINE

Desserts for Your Sweet Tooth

There's more to dessert than ice cream, College Man, although ice cream is a good start. Buying boxed cake mixes and brownie mixes? I have no problem with that - when they're on sale they run about a dollar a box. You usually have to have oil and eggs on hand to add to the mix. A box of cake mix usually makes about 24 cupcakes which could actually last you and your roommates a day or two. You use a 12-cup capacity muffin tin to make the cupcakes but the secret to practically zero cleanup is buying the cupcake liners that you put in before you pour in the cupcake batter. And only filled the cupcake liners about half full with the batter otherwise the cupcakes get out of control and can spill over the edge while baking. The icing is where the effort comes in - buttercream frosting is the best: 1 stick softened butter, 2 cups sifted powdered sugar, 2 teaspoons vanilla extract and 2-3 tablespoons milk and mix it with a hand mixer until smooth and you're good to go! That's enough for 24 cupcakes.

Banana Splitsville

SERVES 4

4 ripe peeled bananas
½ gallon of your favorite ice cream
Whipped cream
Salted peanuts
Chocolate syrup or caramel sauce
Peanut butter cups

Great after a breakup!

Cut bananas in half lengthwise and arrange in the bottom of a bowl. Top with ice cream with the all toppings!

Bananas Foster

SERVES 6

6 tablespoons butter
1 cup dark brown sugar
¼ cup dark rum
1 teaspoon vanilla extract
½ teaspoon cinnamon
4 peeled ripe bananas
Vanilla ice cream (*or whipped cream*)

Bananas Foster was created in the 1950's in New Orleans at the well-known Brennan's Restaurant, supposedly for a very regular customer named Richard Foster. Desserts that are traditionally meant to be flambéed (yes, lit on fire – for those of you with pyromania tendencies or actual history, definitely skip this part) are best left to chefs in commercial kitchens so we're NOT recommending flaming it with rum – it's in there already!

Melt butter, brown sugar, rum, vanilla extract and cinnamon in a heavy, large skillet on low heat, stirring occasionally, until bubbly. Slice bananas lengthwise, then crosswise twice (makes 4 pieces per banana). Add to skillet, coating bananas well in the mixture and sauté on medium-high heat for 2-3 minutes, stirring constantly. The bananas will soften at this point but will still maintain their shape. Remove from the heat. Spoon warm bananas into serving bowls, pour remaining sauce over the bananas then top with a scoop of vanilla ice cream.

Chili Chocolate Fondue

SERVES 4

1 cup heavy cream
2 cups (10-ounce bag) dark, milk chocolate or cinnamon chips
½ teaspoon cinnamon (*skip this if you use cinnamon chips!*)
½ chili powder or you can add orange zest too

WHAT TO DIP IN THE FONDUE:
Small strawberries, apple chunks, dried fruits, sliced bananas, small cookies, miniature marshmallows, and if you run out you can always even dip nacho chips and most anything because it's dipped in chocolate!

In a medium heavy pot, heat the heavy cream over medium heat stirring occasionally, using a whisk, until very hot but not boiling. Stir in the chocolate chips until melted, giving it one last whisking to make sure all the chocolate is melted. Turn off the heat and remove pot from burner. Use forks or chops sticks to pierce the fruit and dip into the chocolate fondue! If the chocolate starts to get too thick, just add a few tablespoons of heavy cream and heat for a minute or two, whisk it and it will have the right consistency again! Happy Valentine's Day people!

Coca-Cola Cake

SERVES 9

CAKE:

Preheat oven to 350°. Pour milk into a cup then stir in the lemon juice – allow to sit for 5 minutes –you will see the milk beginning to thicken. In a medium bowl, combine Coca-Cola, milk, butter, sugar, honey graham crumbs, eggs, vanilla extract, flour, baking soda and black pepper. Using your hand mixer, beat at low speed until well incorporated or if you don't have a hand mixer, beat with a spoon or a whisk. Pour batter into a greased and floured 8" x 8" inch pan. Bake for 30-35 minutes or until a kitchen knife inserted comes out clean. Remove from the oven then poke holes all over the top of the cake with a fork.

FROSTING:

Combine butter, melted chocolate, Coca-Cola, powdered sugar and vanilla extract in a mixer and beat until smooth. Pour frosting over warm cake so it soaks in.

CAKE:

½ cup milk
1 tablespoon lemon juice or white or apple cider vinegar
1 cup Coca-Cola
1 stick softened butter
1 cup sugar
4 honey graham crackers, processed into crumbs or well-crushed
2 large eggs
2 teaspoons vanilla extract
2 cups all-purpose flour
1 teaspoon baking soda
1 teaspoon black pepper

FROSTING:

½ stick butter, softened
2 ounces melted unsweetened dark baking chocolate (or whatever chocolate you have)
½ cup Coca-Cola
(1) 16-ounce package sifted powdered sugar
1 tablespoon vanilla extract

No-Bake Lime Cheesecake

SERVES 6

Your mini food processor and hand mixer will come in handy on this one!

Break up graham crackers and place in the mini food processor - if too much, do it in two batches. Pulse until crumbled. Remove and place in a medium bowl, stir in sugar and melted butter and mix well. Press mixture into a pie plate using your fingers or the back of a spoon.

Using your hand mixer, whip the heavy cream until stiff then beat in the cream cheese, powdered sugar and vanilla until smooth. Spread the cream cheese mixture into the pie crust. Ready to eat now, but you can also cover it and refrigerate for later!

CRUST:

4 graham crackers
¼ cup sugar
½ stick melted butter
Zest of 1 lime

FILLING:

1 pint heavy or whipping cream
8 ounces softened cream cheese
3 tablespoons powdered sugar
1 teaspoon vanilla extract
Juice of 1 lime

No-Crust Apple Pie

SERVES 4-6

4 peeled and cored apples
Juice of 1 lemon
Zest of 1 lemon
½ cup sugar
1 teaspoon cinnamon
2 tablespoons all-purpose flour
2 tablespoons butter, cut into little pieces
½ glass of liquid, like a leftover margarita, apple juice, or any fruit juice or even water
8" x 8" baking dish

Preheat oven to 350°. Butter an 8" x 8" baking dish or casserole dish similar in size. Slice the apples thin, about ¼". Once all the apples are nestled in the baking dish, sprinkle with lemon juice then take the lemon rind and zest it, and sprinkle it over the apples. The zest can sometimes get stuck on the inside of the zester, so just make sure that it's not sticking. Sprinkle the sugar, cinnamon, flour, butter pieces and liquid of your choice over the apples. Bake for 30-40 minutes or until bubbly and the apples are soft.

Peanut Butter Cookies

MAKES 24 COOKIES

2 cups crunchy or smooth peanut butter
1 cup sugar
1½ cups all-purpose flour
2 beaten eggs
1 teaspoon vanilla extract
1 teaspoon salt

Preheat oven to 350°. Combine all ingredients in a medium bowl and stir until dough forms. Using your hands, roll cookie dough into 24 balls and arrange them on an ungreased cookie sheet. Press down slightly on each cookie with the palm of your hand or press it down using the back of a fork. Stick the cookie sheet in the freezer for 10 minutes. Bake for 18-20 minutes. Allow to cool or they will crumble!

Rum & Coke Apple Mini-Cakes

MAKES 24 MINI-CAKES

½ cup spiced or dark rum
½ cup Coca-Cola
1 ½ cups all-purpose flour
1 cup instant oatmeal (dry, not made)
1 cup sugar
1 ½ teaspoons baking soda
1 ½ teaspoons cinnamon
2 eggs
2 peeled, cored and coarsely chopped apples
1 stick melted butter
1 teaspoon salt
½ teaspoon black pepper
Cooking spray with flour*
***or you can oil and flour the tins**
12-cup capacity muffin tin

Preheat oven to 325°. Put all ingredients into a large bowl and stir until well incorporated. Spray a 12-cup capacity muffin tin with cooking spray with flour. Fill the muffin tins half-full with batter – this will require two batches. Bake for 20 minutes or until a knife inserted into the center comes out clean. You will need to wash, thoroughly dry and re-spray the muffin tins for the second batch of mini-cakes – if you don't do this, they will stick big time!

SERVES 8

S'mores (Oven Baked)

1/3 stick melted butter
8 graham crackers, broken into pieces
4 chocolate bars, broken into pieces
1 cup chocolate syrup
40 large marshmallows
8" x 8" baking dish

Preheat oven to 400°. Fill baking dish with melted butter, pieces of graham cracker, pieces of chocolate bars, and chocolate syrup. Bake for 5 minutes. Remove from oven and add marshmallows. Return to oven and continue to bake for 5 minutes or until the marshmallows begin to turn a light golden brown on top. DO NOT LEAVE IT UNATTENDED while baking -it could be a fire hazard! Remove and allow to cool for a few minutes before serving.

SERVES 6

Tropical Apple Brown Betty

6 granny smith apples
1 cup applesauce
1 teaspoon cinnamon
Juice of 1 orange juice (or ¼ cup orange juice)
Juice of 1 lemon or lime (or 1 tablespoon lemon juice)
½ cup all-purpose flour
½ cup light or dark brown sugar
½ stick butter
½ teaspoon salt

8" x 8" baking dish, lightly buttered

Preheat oven to 350°. Peel, core and slice apples, then place in a medium bowl. Stir in applesauce, cinnamon, orange juice and lemon juice, coating apples well. In another medium bowl, combine flour, brown sugar, butter and salt. Cut with two knives until the butter is the size of small peas. Pour apple slices and liquid into baking dish, then sprinkle with flour mixture. Bake for 45 minutes or until bubbly. If you like a really crispy topping, broil for 1 minute – watch carefully so it doesn't burn!

Notes:

What Belongs To Who? Or To Whom?!?! Sharing The Fridge

This can be one of the most annoying aspects of living with a group of guys. Coming into the kitchen looking forward to something that you bought at the grocery store earlier... and it's not there. We all know that we do it, just take one of our roommate's pantry or fridge items every once in a while because you're waaaaay too lazy to go all the way to the grocery store. So my roommates and I have figured out a much easier and less time consuming method of making sure your food does not get 'borrowed' by one of your roommates. All you have to do is designate the shelves and drawers of the refrigerator and pantry. It may seem obvious, but many college men don't do this and not only does it help organize your food, but it also gives you an accurate estimate of how long until you need to go to the grocery store...again. And when you're there, don't forget to replace what you 'borrowed'.

Signature Dishes? Me?

Signature dishes are the ones you will become known for amongst your roommates and friends - they don't have to be fancy or complicated - they just have to be good and consistent. So a great way to plan your signature dishes is to begin with making recipes that you love - what is your favorite? Pasta? Chicken? Fish? Veggies? Something more exotic? The choices are endless and it takes only a few ingredients – simple mashed potatoes make great signature dishes. A Grilled PB & J makes a great signature dish. A baked chicken makes a great signature dish. Eventually you will master a few recipes and like a DJ, you will get requests!

The Dishwasher is Your Friend

My aunt Mary puts everything in the dishwasher including pots and pans. I think she would put my little cousins in there if she could, just to get them extra clean! You can put most plastic and glass cutting boards in the dishwasher (as long as they are not wood, as they will warp). And if you are out of dishwasher soap, DO NOT try what I my mom did once. She put liquid dish soap in the little compartment inside the dishwasher door and it was a HUGE soapy mess, with bubbles everywhere and the dishes were STILL dirty. And not everybody has a dishwasher, so if that is the case, just use the hottest water that you can tolerate and lots of soap when you wash your dishes!

Storing Leftovers

"Leftovers" is one of those words that has an unappealing connotation to some, but there is magic and leftovers. A refrigerated 2-day old leftover baked potato, looking shriveled and rubbery in its brown skin can come to life again once peeled, sprinkle with capers, olive oil, salt and pepper. Or top it with a poached egg sprinkle with fresh parsley, it stands on its own, making a comeback like an actress coming back in her golden years! Rice can spring back to life when placed in a bowl, to which steaming vegetable or chicken broth has been added, sprinkle with sliced green onions and red chili pepper flakes-a new mail is born. How to store leftovers? Transfer leftovers to an airtight container and refrigerate or wrap in foil or clear food wrap. I think you can handle - it's pretty straightforward, College Man. Making sure leftovers or properly refrigerated is key to food safety. Most leftovers should be eaten within 2-3 days. Sometimes a dish taste even better the second day when the flavors have had time to meld, unless of course it's a sandwich then it's probably a soggy mess and you need to have eaten it yesterday...

CHAPTER TEN

Impress the Rents

When parents come to town, we College Men expect to be wined and dined, so why not cut your 'rents a break and make a few appetizers - sort of like tailgating before the big event which in this case is dinner at a real restaurant - maybe even one with white table cloths! And if you and your roommates are worried about the state of your apartment, figure out a barter with somebody and have him clean it up in exchange for tutoring, detailing his car or how about COOKING him a dinner (or six) depending on the sweat equity involved in making the place presentable.

The Roasted Grape Tomatoes in this chapter are delicious heaped on top of the Lemon Hummus with toasted pita wedges. Guacamole isn't a dip that can be made too far in advance - about 30 minutes at the most. The store bought guac can last for weeks in the fridge because its packaging is designed that way. But the ingredients can be prepared in advance - you can chop the tomatoes and squeeze the fresh lime juice, so putting it all together does not take more than 5 minutes once you're ready to make it. A platter of Dried Apricots with Blue Cheese is super simple to make using only three ingredients! If you run out of time, just grab a bunch of red grapes, a bunch of green grapes, some interesting cheese like a creamy St. Andre (creamier than Brie) or whatever looks good that's on sale and some fresh crackers. Arrange them on the largest plate around with a knife and wait for the "oooohs" and the "aaaaahs" and then make sure to be on time for the reservations!

Cinnamon Chip Brownies

½ stick melted butter
½ cup vegetable or
    coconut oil
1 cup sugar
1 teaspoon vanilla extract
2 eggs
1 cup all-purpose flour
1 cup cocoa powder
    *(or 6 of the hot chocolate
    mix individual packets)*
½ teaspoon salt
½ cup cinnamon chips
    *(or sprinkle ½ teaspoon
    cinnamon over chocolate
    chips)*
Cooking spray

Brownies remind me of my grandmother – soft and sweet on the inside and crinkly on the outside. Just kidding, Grandmom, I love you!

Preheat oven to 325°. Spray the pan lightly with cooking spray or you can oil it with vegetable oil using a paper towel or your fingers, then line it with foil. Mix all ingredients together in a bowl except the cinnamon chips, using your hand mixer or a large spoon. Spread the brownie batter evenly in the pan. Sprinkle the cinnamon chips over the top of the batter. Bake for 35 minutes or until a knife inserted in the center comes out clean. Even if a tiny bit of batter sticks to the knife, take them out of the oven and let them sit until they cool down a bit-don't risk over baking them! If you allow them to cool down a bit (10-15 minutes) they will stay together much better when you cut into them, but if you are eating them right out of the pan with your hands I guess it doesn't really matter.

Important: This is the thing - you need to use an 8"x 8" metal or glass baking dish because then the brownies with be nice and thick. If you use a larger size pan, the brownies will be thinner and will be more prone to be overbaked, dry and even burned around the edges.

Coconut Garlic Green Beans

1 pound green beans
½ cup water
1 tablespoon coconut oil
6 cloves chopped garlic
½ teaspoon salt

Snap the ends off the green beans them place them in a medium skillet with the water, cover and bring to a boil over medium heat. Cook for 3 minutes, remove the beans from the skillet, and set them aside in a bowl. Heat 1 tablespoon coconut oil in the skillet and add chopped garlic, stirring for 2-3 minutes. Stir in green beans, add salt and stir fry for 5 minutes. Cover until ready to serve.

Dried Apricots Stuffed with Blue Cheese

4 ounces crumbled blue
    cheese
32 dried apricots
    (12-16 ounces)
4 tablespoons strawberry
    preserves

Slice the dried apricots on the side, creating a "pocket", and stuff with a small amount of blue cheese. Arrange on platter. Nuke strawberry preserves for 30 seconds and drizzle over apricots. Serve with toothpicks.

!Holy Moly Guacamolei

4 ripe avocados
2 ripe chopped tomatoes
1 peeled and diced green apple
⅓ cup fresh lime juice
½ teaspoon salt
¼ teaspoon black pepper
Tortilla chips

Having ripe tomatoes and avocados can make or break this recipe – if they are not ripe, they are ill-prepared and tasteless (like we College Men can be!) Our secret ingredient is green apple – they're cheaper than avocados, add a bit of crunch and a tangy flavor that makes this guacamole super delicious!

Cut avocados in half - there are a huge pits in the middle, so cut around them. Use a spoon to cut around and dislodge the pit and to scrape the avocado flesh from the skins. Scrape out any brown parts. Cut avocados into ½" chunks. Gently stir all the ingredients together, but don't stir too much or it will get mushy. Serve with tortilla chips. Eat on the spot - it starts to turn brown and does not hold up well in the fridge for more than a day.

Jalapeño Tuna Melt in Your Mouth

4 cans (5-ounce size) solid white tuna, packed in water, drained
2 jalapeño peppers, seeded and diced
½ cup sweet relish
6 chopped hard boiled eggs
1 cup mayonnaise
2 tablespoons finely chopped red onion
1 unpeeled, cored and finely chopped apple
Juice of 1 lemon
8 slices tasty bread
Salt & pepper to taste
12 slices white sharp cheddar cheese *(or your favorite cheese)*
Extra sweet or dill pickles

MAKES 8 OPEN FACED TUNA MELTS

When buying canned tuna, the one that is packed in water tastes better than the one in oil. Also, the "solid white" tuna meat is the tastiest. When you open the tuna cans, drain them of any excess liquid before using in a recipe. If you don't have every single ingredient (except the core ingredients like tuna and bread, duh!), don't sweat it. It will still be delicious!

Preheat oven to 400°. Combine tuna, jalapeños, sweet relish, hard boiled eggs, mayonnaise, red onion, apple, lemon juice, salt and pepper in a medium bowl. Arrange bread slices on a large cookie sheet. Divide the tuna mixture in rounded mounds equally between the bread slices, using an ice cream scooper or a large spoon, pressing down so it stays together. Place 2 slices of cheese over each. Bake for 3 minutes or until melted. Transfer to individual serving plates. Serve hot.

Oven-Roasted Chili Peanuts

2 cups dry roasted peanuts
2 tablespoons vegetable oil
2 tablespoons chili sauce
1 teaspoon salt
½ teaspoon black pepper

MAKES 2 CUPS

Preheat the oven to 325°. Arrange peanuts in a lipped baking pan-they should not overlap. Roast for 15-20 minutes, stirring once. Remove from oven and stir in salt and pepper. Immediately, transfer to a flat plate while they cool or eat warm! Trust me – you will eat them warm!

Roasted Grape Tomatoes

2 cups grape tomatoes
4 chopped garlic cloves
1 tablespoon extra-virgin
olive oil
Salt and pepper to taste

Preheat oven to 400°. In medium baking dish large enough to fit tomatoes in a single layer, add garlic and olive oil, and toss gently. Roast for 20-25 minutes or until tomatoes are plump and just starting to burst, stirring once while roasting. Salt and pepper to taste. Serve with toothpicks.

Shrimp with Ricotta Salata

SERVES 6-8 SMALL PLATES

1 pound ricotta salata
(or Parmesan, feta, goat or
white cheddar cheese)
1 pound medium shrimp,
peeled and deveined
6 chopped basil leaves
¼ cup extra-virgin olive oil +
2 tablespoons to reserve
2 cloves garlic
Blackening spice mix
(see page 43 for recipe)

½ cup balsamic vinegar
Salt & pepper to taste
Chopped basil leaves

Toss shrimp with olive oil, minced garlic, chopped basil leaves and blackening spices, or any dried herbs you like in a medium bowl. Heat a heavy skillet and pan sear for 3 minutes a side. Arrange tomato wedges on individual small plates, then drizzle with olive oil, balsamic vinegar, salt, pepper, then add pan seared shrimp. Top with a wedge of ricotta salata and chopped basil.

Wedge Salad with Blue Cheese

SERVES 4

1 head iceberg lettuce, cut into
4 wedges, rinsed, face down
on paper towels
3 ripe tomatoes, each cut into
4 wedges
1 small red onion, sliced into
8 rounds
8 strips uncooked diced bacon

DRESSING:
½ cup mayonnaise
½ cup sour cream
8 ounces crumbled blue cheese
Juice of ½ lemon
1 tablespoon white vinegar or
red wine vinegar
Salt and freshly ground pepper
to taste

In medium skillet over low heat, cook bacon pieces until brown and crispy, about 10 minutes, turning occasionally. Drain on paper towels. On each of 4 large bowls or plates, place a wedge of lettuce, tomatoes around the sides. Arrange sliced onion and cooked bacon on top. Stir together dressing ingredients in a small bowl. Spoon dressing on top.

50 Cent Wings

The best night of the week for College Men. 50 Cent Wings? Are you kidding me?? So you're telling me I can be in a food coma by eating 18 wings for only $9? Done. But what if you could be doing this any night you wanted and not have to wait until the day of the week the restaurant offers it to you? You can and it really isn't that hard. These Whoooa-Sabi Wings will blow you away with an amazing combination of flavor and spice. Give 'em a try and share with friends!

Preheat oven to 375°. In a large bowl, combine honey, light brown sugar, soy sauce, vegetable oil, prepared Wasabi, chopped garlic cloves, orange juice and zest. Add chicken wings to mixture then toss until well coated. Arrange wings on a foil-lined, large, lipped baking sheet so the wings are not overlapping. Bake for 50 minutes, stirring twice while cooking. In a small bowl, stir together sour cream and prepared wasabi sauce. Serve with wings.

Whooooa-Sabi Wings

4 pounds chicken wings, drummettes and flats separated, tips discarded
⅔ cup honey
⅔ cup light brown sugar
⅔ cup soy sauce
¼ cup vegetable oil
6 tablespoons prepared wasabi
4 garlic cloves, finely chopped
Juice of 4 oranges
Zest of 1 orange

DIPPING SAUCE:
1 cup sour cream
½ cup prepared Wasabi sauce

CONGRATULATIONS

Congratulations on having completed the 100 recipes in The College Man's Cookbook — even if you haven't tried all of them, you've got your whole life ahead of you. We hope we have fulfilled our mission that we set out to do: to make the kitchen (and cooking) a less scary place than you may have thought and to make you a College Man who knows his way around the kitchen. And remember that when you've got the confidence to cook without a recipe and to experiment is when you will surprise yourself — and remember to write it down so you'll remember the next time. Creative juices are short-lived sometimes and you might not remember your measurements the next day... Maybe one day, you'll write your own cookbook! In the meantime, cook well and eat well. And enjoy your diploma- we know you're gonna want to hang it on the wall!

TESTIMONIALS

"I never used a cookbook before but my mom left this on my kitchen counter when I moved off campus...it's awesome!
- ZACK

"I'm no chef but The Bad-Ass Godfather Sub is my favorite."
- CHRIS

"Cooking for yourself instead of eating out all the time is fun once you get the hang of it."
- JOHN

"My family always cooked a lot so I'm pretty good with the basics - the late night snacks I've tried so far are delicious."
- RYAN

"I'm the only cook in our apartment and these recipes are easy and inexpensive so I get everybody to chip in and we make a few recipes a week."
- SEAN

"Cooking was never my thing but they made it easy."
- CONNER

"I like these recipes because money is tight and I save a ton by cooking at home. The shopping lists were helpful too."
- ALEX

"My roommates and I use The College Man's Cookbook a lot on the weekends - great tips, too."
- KEVIN

WE AWARD THIS DIPLOMA TO

_____

who has successfully prepared all, some or a few of the recipes in

The College Man's Cookbook or will really try to get around to it when he can.

On this _____ day of _____, in the year _____

QUIDQUID LATINE DICTUM, ALTUM VIDETUR

_____
Carrie Hirsch

_____
George Hirsch, Jr.

ABOUT THE CO-AUTHORS

GEORGE HIRSCH, JR.
George Hirsch, Jr., has been cooking as long as he can remember. He has followed in his mother's footsteps and pursued cooking as a favorite hobby while he worked toward a degree in Sports Management. As a member of the graduating Class of '16 of the University of Georgia, he shared an apartment with five roommates, making him a resident expert in the world of college kitchens. This prompted him to write The College Man's Cookbook – these 100 recipes are meant to be easy for The College Man to prepare in his own kitchen without too much time, money or fuss.

CARRIE HIRSCH
George's mother, Carrie Hirsch, has food on the brain all the time. She worked in fine wine distribution and as a sales manager for national companies including Applegate Farms and Les Trois Petits Cochons Pate Company. Since 2005, she has been a food editor and columnist and creates recipes for magazines and newspapers. She likes to say that her son George Hirsch, Jr. was born with a wooden spoon in his mouth... he spent most of his youth in the kitchen. Creating, testing and collaborating with George and her husband Butch on The College Man's Cookbook was a lot of work that brought her joy.

ABOUT THE PHOTOGRAPHER

BUTCH HIRSCH
Butch Hirsch established his photography studio in Manhattan's Chelsea neighborhood in the 1980's where he shot editorial for numerous magazines including *Vogue* (European), *L'Officiel*, and *Elle* during his career as a successful fashion and beauty photographer. He has photographed numerous artists, musicians, athletes including Amiri Farris, Neil Young, Ivan Lendl, Dan Driessen, Arthur Blank, Jesse Blanco, and Chef Sallie Ann Robinson. Shooting guacamole and mac n cheese was easy – they don't talk back and there's much less drama!

ACKNOWLEDGMENTS FROM CARRIE HIRSCH

A special thanks to my Mom (and Dad, but he burned a lot of toast) for cooking delicious meals at home, mostly from scratch, for our large family so I was inspired to continue the tradition. And to Sherri Lonz for her keen eye, outstanding graphic talent and for supporting us throughout the layout process - you are a true friend. And thank you to William N. Iles who did the voice over for the cookbook video trailer - you're an amazing talent with a great voice and perfect comedic timing. I appreciate you, Jesse Blanco, and thank you for all you do to promote the food scene and for writing the foreword. And thanks to Judy for helping with the tedious job of proofing! To my husband, Butch, who is always game to taste new recipes and who contributed his beautiful food shots, and to my sons Julian and co-author George, Jr. who spent a good part of their lives in the kitchen bonding and cooking with me and continue to do so. I am honored to have learned so much about food and the joy it brings from the inimitable Chef Eric Sayers and my dear friend and cookbook author Sallie Ann Robinson – both supremely dedicated, successful and passionate about everything they do in and out of the kitchen. And to my sister Mary who is the best cook I know – thanks for all the memorable meals and all the love we've shared over the years. It's especially satisfying to cook for those who appreciate the work involved.

A special thanks to Harris Teeter!

Made in the USA
Las Vegas, NV
20 December 2020